THE BOOK OF
SCHMALTZ

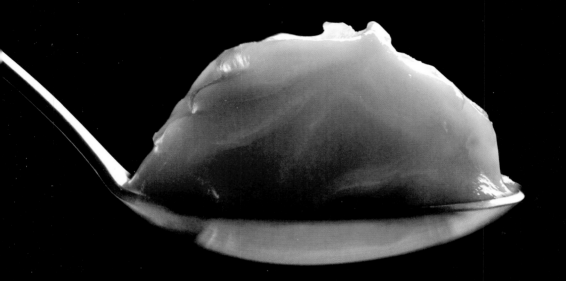

THE BOOK OF
SCHMALTZ

• Love Song to a Forgotten Fat •

MICHAEL RUHLMAN

PHOTOGRAPHS BY DONNA TURNER RUHLMAN

LITTLE, BROWN AND COMPANY

NEW YORK   BOSTON   LONDON

Little, Brown and Company
Hachette Book Group
237 Park Avenue, New York, NY 10017
littlebrown.com

First Edition: August 2013

Little, Brown and Company is a division of Hachette Book Group, Inc.
The Little, Brown name and logo are trademarks of Hachette Book Group, Inc.

The publisher is not responsible for websites (or their
content) that are not owned by the publisher.

The Hachette Speakers Bureau provides a wide range of authors for speaking
events. To find out more, go to hachettespeakersbureau.com or call (866) 376-6591.

ISBN 978-0-316-25408-3

Library of Congress Control Number 2013935272

10 9 8 7 6 5 4 3 2 1

WOR

Printed in the United States of America

To Lois Waxman Baron and her forebears

THE BOOK OF
SCHMALTZ
A LOVE SONG TO A FORGOTTEN FAT

THE BOOK OF
SCHMALTZ

"A Thread in a Great Tapestry"

"There's nothing else like it," Lois Baron lamented one afternoon at a neighborhood gathering. "It's a shame we're losing it."

"It," uttered softly, almost apologetically, was schmaltz.

Lois is a terrific cook and was looking forward to all the cooking she was planning as Rosh Hashanah and Yom Kippur, the High Holy Days of the Jewish year, approached. First on her list was schmaltz, the rendered chicken fat, cooked with onion, that would flavor so many of her dishes.

I'd longed to work with this neglected, much-maligned, all-but-forgotten fat, and that remark catalyzed the urge.

I have for years been a pro-fat proselytizer in a fat-phobic land, singing the glories of pig fat, working assiduously to encourage America to make sausage in the book *Charcuterie*, and to dry-cure salami and prosciutto in the book *Salumi*. And I rail against America's knee-jerk vilifying of fat generally. Fat doesn't make us fat—eating too much makes us fat. Eating all that processed crap, and cleaning our overfilled plates at chain restaurants, makes us fat. Lack of vigorous daily exercise makes us fat.

The truth is, our bodies need fat. Fat is stored energy. Fat allows our bodies to absorb fat-soluble vitamins as well as fatty acids that our bodies don't produce. Eating calorie-dense meat and fat is likely the reason the brains of our early ancestors grew huge and our bodies became healthy and our genes spread.

Fat—in the form of back fat from well-raised pigs, rendered fat from pasture-raised chickens, butter, small-batch olive oil from a good Californian or Italian orchard—is good. Fat in its many forms adds extraordinary flavor and succulence to our food.

Fat is not something to fear. It's all about balance: a diet including lots and lots of vegetables along with moderate amounts of grains and meats and dairy products, combined with plenty of exercise. But you already know this. You know how you feel when you live that way: good. You know how you

feel when you don't, when you polish off a heaping dinner plate at the Cheesecake Factory followed by its namesake dessert: stuffed, uncomfortable. Listen to your body and use your common sense.

Never in my experience, though, is this railing against fat more forcefully voiced than when Jews talk about schmaltz. Schmaltz cannot be uttered without someone talking about clogged arteries and an early grave. There's Jewish guilt, which is such a powerful emotion that even a goy such as myself is afflicted, and then right behind it is Fear of Schmaltz.

The word itself even sounds bad. Moreover, it has entered our language as a derogatory term for a creative work that is overly sentimental. My Webster's *New World Dictionary* gives this definition *only*. The schmaltz we cook with doesn't even *exist* in the English language, according to this source.

I am here to say: Schmaltz Is Good, and Schmaltz Is Great. You really haven't experienced a potato pancake until you've had one sautéed in schmaltz. Onions sautéed in schmaltz are a powerful flavoring tool. Schmaltz can replace butter in baked goods for extraordinary effects.

My goal here is not simply to give schmaltz back, guilt-free, to the Jews, but to give it to American home cooks far and wide. Making use of chicken fat in your cooking not only enriches your cooking, it's right from an economical and ethical standpoint as well, in that you make use of something instead of throwing it out. Chefs call it total utilization. This means that if you roast a whole chicken for dinner, use the carcass to make soup for another night (include the neck and gizzard for this as well) and save the fat (either raw, pulled from the bird before roasting and then rendered, or the rendered fat left in the pan after roasting) to use to season the reserved liver, chopped. Your food will taste better and you avoid waste.

This, after all, was part of how humans became human and managed to stay that way—by cooking food and making sure there was enough to go around. Throughout most of human history, food was not ubiquitous. Taking advantage of every consumable gram of food was once the main work of hearth and home. This is still the case even today in parts of the developing world. We forget this at our peril.

Until the 1900s, you couldn't just go out and buy a jug of vegetable oil to cook with. Most people had to rely on animal fat—butter from the cow and lard from the pig. Beef fat was also used, but pigs were abundant and more manageable, so lard dominated until 1911, when Procter & Gamble figured out how to turn pressed cottonseed oil into a lard-like substance by hydrogenating it.

Some religions, of course, forbid eating anything porcine. Jews in the Middle East had ready access to olive oil, but in the colder latitudes, the Ashkenazi Jews relied on poultry fat for their cooking, and it was this fat that came to characterize traditional

Jewish cuisine.* No old culture exists without a cuisine. As the pogroms and persecution that have forever dogged and dislocated Jews pushed them in the 19th and 20th centuries to the burgeoning United States of America, their cuisine came with them.

And like all cuisines that arrived here, the best of each became homogenized and mass-produced so that what we have now is scarcely recognizable from what it was. Consider pepperoni pizza, Bud Lite, and Kraft singles. And, germane to our subject here, Vlasic dill pickles, frozen latkes, bagel-shaped supermarket rolls (no, they're *not* bagels), and jarred matzo balls.

I would argue, though, that because immigrants often turn first to selling food in their new environment (a low-capital, high-labor business venture), and because American Jews were among the most insular of immigrant cultures due to strict religious rules, the food they sold stayed mainly within their communities and thus remained less adulterated than other cuisines (remember that chop suey was once the defining dish of Chinese cuisine in the United States). As the Jews fled and dispersed, food was one way to bind their community and to help them remain attached to one another, even at a distance.

So, as other cultures grew increasingly assimilated, happily, the Jewish food shops remained true to their cuisines. French charcuteries and Italian salumerias, unprotected by any

---

*There is every reason to believe that turkey schmaltz would have been a part of Jewish cuisine had turkeys existed in Europe, or had Jews existed in America along with Native Americans. The turkey, as Ben Franklin pointed out when arguing for its being elevated to our national bird, is native to North America. And turkey schmaltz is every bit as valuable as schmaltz made from chicken fat. Indeed, it's turkey schmaltz that I use to make the roux for our Thanksgiving gravy.

religious strictures, died out as Oscar Mayer and other food processors steamrolled the country. Thus we still have great pastrami and corned beef, lox and bagels, pickled herring and chopped liver, and other treasured staples of the Jewish American delicatessen, but most of our salami is cooked rather than cured, and the great mortadella of Bologna has become a baloney sandwich on Wonder Bread.

And just as American chefs and home cooks have only recently discovered the age-old crafts of charcuterie and salumi, so too should we look to Jewish cuisine to preserve what might be lost. Charcuterie and salumi are largely defined by a specific animal and its fat; it's likewise logical, then, to focus our attention not on the entirety of Jewish cuisine but rather on the animal and the fat that define this distinctive branch of it.

"Schmaltz is like a thread that runs through a great tapestry," said Lois, my neighbor and portal into the fabulous world of schmaltz, one evening on the porch of her home in Cleveland Heights, Ohio. "It's a secret handshake among Jews who love to cook and eat."

The Book of Schmaltz intends to pull out that thread and hold it up to the light, and to spread that handshake among all cooks who care about great food and great cooking.

What follows is a primer on schmaltz, one that will reexamine traditional Jewish dishes (kugel, kishke, and kreplach) as well as offer ideas for contemporary recipes that take advantage of the great flavor and versatility of this wonderful fat.

I'll first describe the steps in making your own schmaltz and look at differing schools of schmaltz thought, then follow with two dozen benchmark recipes that explore the various uses of schmaltz—and, I hope, pave the way for your own variations and put schmaltz permanently into your arsenal of cooking tools.

I'm not advocating that you turn your kitchen into a year-round schmaltz factory, that you cook everything in schmaltz. And I do, of course, recommend a diet with an abundance of vegetables and moderate portions of high-calorie foods with small amounts of animal fats. Foods cooked or enriched with schmaltz should be a special treat, something cherished and rare.

Because the fact is this: nothing tastes like schmaltz. It's utterly unique, with an aromatic savoriness as distinctive as a great olive oil. In the same way that there is no substitute for the aroma of a truffle, that nothing smells or tastes quite like it, so too does schmaltz add flavor and richness to a range of preparations that simply cannot be imitated or reproduced any other way. Potatoes take on a crispness and taste that vegetable oil can't produce. Meats and starches enriched with schmaltz have a depth and complexity that put them on a different spectrum from those same foods prepared with olive oil or butter.

As Lois rightly says, "There is *nothing* like schmaltz."

THE KOSHER QUESTION

Most of these recipes are kosher but not all. Presumably, those who keep kosher know for themselves what they can and cannot eat. But I did want to note that three recipes contain dairy: Savory Brioche, Vichyssoise with Gribenes and Chives, and Scones with Roasted Red Pepper and Parmigiano-Reggiano. The brioche can be made kosher by using water instead of milk. I don't recommend making the vichysoisse or the scones without the dairy.

How This Book Came to Be

As I mentioned at the outset, this book began after I heard my neighbor, Lois Baron, waxing poetic on the glories of schmaltz. I'd heard of it but had never cooked with it, and I really didn't know much about how it was used or even made (Lois is adamant that plain rendered chicken fat is not schmaltz—she says that part of what makes schmaltz *schmaltz* is the onion flavor, and I'm inclined to agree).

So I asked her if she wanted to share in this project and teach me how her family has used schmaltz. She laughed, thought I was joking. Who would want a book on this forgotten ingredient and "heart attack food"? I assured her that many would be interested in a book on schmaltz and begged her to please stop talking about it as heart attack food; it doesn't have to be. (Lois is seventy-eight and cooks like a banshee; her husband, Russell, is eighty-three, still practices law, and is a sitting judge for the City of Cleveland Heights; their son is rail-thin; and her daughter is a bike fa-

natic who loves chopped liver.) Lois's mother, born in Russia in 1907, cooked with schmaltz her whole life—even if she wouldn't admit it—and lived to ninety-nine.

Lois agreed and opened her home and kitchen, providing several of the traditional recipes that we used here as a starting point, and she served as a sounding board and adviser throughout the process.

Lois's story is a predominant one among the Jews of the Midwest, Ashkenazi Jews from Russia and Eastern Europe. Lois's grandparents escaped the pogroms along the Russia-Poland border, arriving in Cleveland, where relatives had settled, in 1912.

Lois was born in 1935 and lived on Orville Avenue a couple of blocks north of East 105th Street. Today this street is part of the sterile landscape of the Cleveland Clinic (the state's second largest employer after Wal-Mart). But when Lois was a child, this street was considered to be a second downtown, a thriving commercial and entertainment district.

It contained one place of horror, though—horror to Lois, at least. Lois's mom brought her along to Leizer's chicken store each week when she went for chicken. Leizer's was a typical chicken store of that era, a glass-case retail area in front and chicken coops out back. Her mother would pick out a chicken. The butcher would cut its head off, drain the blood according to Jewish law, remove the feathers, and eviscerate the bird. If they were lucky, they'd find eggs still in the reproductive tract, delicacies they'd drop into the chicken soup made from the hen. Her mother would save all the skin and fat to make the schmaltz.*

Lois was a girl during World War II and remembers it as a happy time in that it brought the community together. Food was central. Eastern European Jewish cuisine, Lois reminded me, was born of poverty and the ghettos, so it remains a cuisine of simplicity, cuisine of the home. Restaurants were nonexistent in shtetls, of course, and many homes didn't have their own ovens. Families relied on the local bakery to cook their Sabbath food, such as cholent, in the oven, banked for the night.

In the 1940s in the Midwest, food was likewise basic. They were poor, but the children didn't know it, Lois says, because they always had enough

---

*Part of the reason schmaltz fell by the wayside likely has to do with today's commercial farming. We've created breeds of chicken that grow so fast, just six weeks from hatched to dispatched, that they scarcely have time to develop the kind of fat Lois's mom could get from what she bought at Leizer's, old fat hens that were no longer reliable layers. And this is likely why they were rarely roasted, almost always stewed or used for soup to tenderize them. And six-week-old four-pound chickens don't start producing eggs by the time they're slaughtered, so no more lovely golden morsels to add to the pot—losses unknown to most today as a result of America's hunger for fast food.

to eat. No one cooked with herbs. Paprika, salt, and pepper were the primary seasonings. Fish was canned tuna, canned salmon, or fresh whitefish and carp from Lake Erie. In the winter they lived on root vegetables; head lettuce and cabbage were the only green vegetables to be had during the long Cleveland winters. They were reform Jews, so Lois's mom coated the chicken with kosher salt to draw out blood, but they didn't *keep* kosher. They celebrated Jewish holidays and had a big dinner on Friday evening to usher in the Sabbath, but, as Lois says, "We drank milk on the Sabbath with our brisket and God didn't smite us dead." And they held on to their traditional dishes, heavy on braised and roasted meats and poultry, eggs and matzo meal, buckwheat groats called kasha, noodles and potatoes, all of it threaded together by schmaltz.

Lois grew up to study Shakespeare (one dissertation short of her Ph.D., sidetracked by schmaltz—and having three college-age children), then became head of public affairs for Saint Luke's Hospital. On summer evenings, I'll often run into Russell, walking George, and we'll talk neighborhood gossip while our dogs chase each other through the honeysuckle groundcover of our leafy suburban street.

These days, of course, conversation often comes back around to schmaltz, and I'm never sorry when it does.

How to Make

SCHMALTZ

Schmaltz can be made with any amount of skin and fat. The butcher or farmer you buy your chicken from will often save skin and fat for you on request. If you like to make chicken soup, save all the skin and fat before you put the bird in the pot. If you roast a chicken regularly, you can pull loose fat from it and trim unused skin, saving it in the freezer until you have enough to render for schmaltz.

Or, as I suggest here, you can use the skin from packaged chicken thighs, which are widely available, reserving the skinless thighs for other uses.

Chop the skin and fat well. This is easiest if it's frozen or partially frozen. The finer you chop the skin, the more efficiently it will render. The skin—connective tissue composed mainly of protein—will eventually become gribenes (cracklings), marvelously flavorful browned bits of crispy skin interspersed with caramelized onion, that serve as a fabulous garnish on anything from tossed salad to chopped liver to matzo balls.

Put the skin and fat in a medium saucepan (nonstick, if you have one) with the water and bring to a simmer over high heat. Turn the burner to low and allow the fat to render. This will take anywhere from 90 minutes to several hours, depending on how much skin and fat you have and how hot your burner is. Give the skin a stir now and then so that it doesn't stick to the bottom and burn. Keep an eye on it. You don't want to let the fat get too hot and turn brown, which will happen once the water has cooked out of the skin. One of the keys to superlative schmaltz is avoiding a roasted flavor and an overly browned appearance; you want a light, clear, clean schmaltz.

When the chicken skin is golden brown, add the onion. Continue to cook until the skin and onion are well browned. The gribenes should be crispy-chewy.

Pour the finished schmaltz fat through a fine-mesh strainer; if you want very clear fat, line the strainer with cheesecloth or a reusable All-

Strain Cloth. Store the gribenes (the onion and cracklings) in a paper towel–lined bowl, covered. Allow the schmaltz to cool, then transfer it to a container, cover, and refrigerate.

Schmaltz will keep for about a week in the fridge, but the sweet, chickeny-oniony fragrance is volatile and will diminish if forgotten behind the week's leftovers. I recommend freezing any schmaltz you won't be using in a day or two. It's best kept in a container, with plastic wrap pressed down onto the surface, covered with a lid or a second layer of plastic wrap, then wrapped in foil if you intend to store for a long time; this careful wrapping prevents other freezer flavors from infiltrating your schmaltz, and the foil will prevent light from damaging the fat over time. Lois recommends freezing schmaltz in 1½-cup/320-milliliter mason jars with rubber seals.

SKIN AND FAT FROM 8 CHICKEN THIGHS (OR 2 CUPS/450 GRAMS MISCELLANEOUS RESERVED CHICKEN SKIN AND FAT)

¼ CUP/60 MILLILITERS WATER

1 SPANISH ONION, CUT INTO MEDIUM DICE

YIELD: ½ CUP/120 GRAMS SCHMALTZ AND ½ CUP/60 GRAMS GRIBENES

Schmaltz

Many cities have kosher butchers. Kosher butchers often sell schmaltz (though Lois and I warn that it will not likely have the onion flavor of the version on page 12). They also often reserve chicken skin and fat that can be purchased for rendering. If you buy schmaltz, you can improve the flavor by cooking more skin and onion in it, till everything is browned; this will result in better schmaltz and valuable gribenes.

In Cleveland we have plentiful farmers' markets where farm-raised chickens and eggs are sold. If your city does, too, ask the farmer to reserve skin and fat for you. They often remove it anyway and are happy to accommodate special orders. This is also the best means of finding fresh chicken livers, which are essential to excellent chopped liver.

Make roast chicken once a week. Before you roast it, pull off all the fat you see and trim all the skin you won't need, including the back skin. Store the fat and skin in the freezer, and in a month or two, you'll have plenty to render for schmaltz. Be sure to reserve the liquid fat left in the pan after roasting your chicken to make the *Pâté de Foie Gras en Terrine* (page 107) or the Roasted Potatoes with Onion and Rosemary (page 111).

Make chicken soup using a whole chicken, removing the skin and visible fat from the chicken before adding the chicken to the pot.

You can make plain schmaltz, but since the onion flavor is so wonderful and so easy to include, why bother?

In my peregrinations, I've heard of only one variation on onion-accented schmaltz. A woman in Chicago said that her family always used garlic and paprika in theirs. That certainly sounds to me like a fine way to flavor it.

You can do all kinds of things to schmaltz to spice it up—for instance, cooking dried chiles in it or adding star anise or Chinese five-spice powder—but we're sticking to the basics here: traditional rendered chicken fat with onion.

I. Cook the chopped chicken fat and skin in a small amount of water to begin the rendering at a gentle temperature. →

2. Once the water and the moisture in the fat and skin have cooked off, the fat can rise above 212°F/100°C and the browning can begin. →

3. When the skin is lightly browned and plenty of fat has been rendered, add the chopped onion. →

4. Be careful not to overcook the fat. It should remain clear and yellow, not brown with an overly roasted flavor. →

5. The browned skin and onion, called gribenes, are a delicious by-product of making schmaltz. →

6. Strain the fat and reserve the gribenes. The schmaltz is ready to use, to refrigerate for up to a week, or to freeze. The gribenes should also be refrigerated or frozen.

Traditional Recipes

I am fascinated by Jewish culture and cuisine, and often astonished by the odd and complex culinary rules, some about slaughtering animals in a certain fashion and others requiring you to bury your flatware. I'm deeply respectful of a culture that has brought so much, well, culture to America, in all facets of life, making an impact far greater than their numbers would lead anyone to forecast. Could it be the food? I won't say no. Cuisine based on poverty, rootlessness, and persecution cannot be expected to be four-star cuisine. But one thing that it has always done is bind families and communities together, and perhaps no other religion links food so powerfully to its holidays.

I am a culinary traditionalist, by which I mean that I use tradition as a primary guide; I believe that "traditional" dishes became that way for a reason, namely that they were meaningful on many different levels—technique, economy, flavor, and often symbolism. That said, everyone has their own way of doing things, and there are no culinary absolutes.

The following recipes I chose for their reliance on schmaltz. Lois was my guide and chief taster. I always referenced other recipes when creating these, comparing and contrasting and always, when possible, keeping it simple and economical. The books I returned to again and again for information and guidance are those by the preeminent writers on the subject of Jewish cuisine, Joan Nathan and Arthur Schwartz. Specifically, I highly recommend Nathan's *Jewish Cooking in America* and Schwartz's *Jewish Home Cooking*. (You'll see both mentioned throughout this book.)

Classic Chicken Soup with Matzo Balls
(aka Mr. Fluffies, page 24)

Traditional Chopped Liver
(page 28)

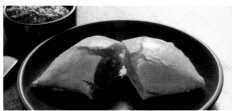

Egg and Gribenes Spread
(page 32)

Potato Kugel
(page 36)

The Mighty Knish
(page 40)

Kreplach (with braised cabbage,
page 55)

Kishke
(page 67)

Helzel
(page 73)

Cholent (page 81)

Classic Chicken Soup with Matzo Balls
(aka Mr. Fluffies)

These matzo balls are traditional in that they use schmaltz in the matzo, and nontraditional in that they also use baking powder. Lois follows Joan Nathan's practice of adding seltzer water, presumably for leavening. But Lois (like Joan) also leaves her matzo mixture to sit for hours, by which time the bubbles will have gone flat. I first made matzo balls using pulverized matzo crackers, which works fine. When I tried using Lois's recipe, I added regular water and a teaspoon of baking powder for lightening the matzo. It worked great, for light, fluffy balls.

Classic Chicken Soup with Matzo Balls
(aka Mr. Fluffies)

According to Lois, there's a major dividing line in Jewish culture between the proponents of "Mr. Fluffies" and those who favor "sinkers," believing that matzo balls should be like shot puts. I'm in the fluffy camp; Lois advocates in between— light but with some chew.

Reading about the subject, I came across Arthur Schwartz's recipe; he, too, uses a chemical leavener, explaining that the former owner of Manhattan's famed Second Avenue Deli confided that this was their secret. My standard rule for all leavening is 1 teaspoon/4 grams per 1 cup/150 grams of flour, and that's what I call for here. If you have gribenes, add them to the matzo balls—they make everything taste better. Some people push a small ball of chopped gribenes into the center of each matzo ball, a kind of hidden treasure.

Cooked matzo balls freeze well, either in the soup or individually wrapped. This recipe will serve 8 but can be halved. I usually plan on 1 cup/240 milliliters of chicken soup per serving. I like to add additional vegetables and garnish for flavor, appearance, and nutrition, but all you really need for this soup is good chicken stock and matzo balls.

This is a great, comforting, cold-weather soup. For a more elegant take on matzo balls in soup, see the recipe for Four-Star Matzo Ball Soup (page 101) in the Contemporary Recipes section.

Classic Chicken Soup with Matzo Balls
(aka Mr. Fluffies)

MATZO BALLS:

1 cup/140 grams matzo meal (or 4 squares of matzo, well pulverized in a food processor)

4 large eggs, beaten

¼ cup/60 grams schmaltz, melted

¼ cup/30 grams gribenes (optional)

¼ cup/60 milliliters chicken stock or water

1 teaspoon baking powder

1 teaspoon kosher salt

½ teaspoon freshly ground black pepper

SOUP:

2 tablespoons/30 grams schmaltz (or canola oil if you're low on schmaltz)

1 Spanish onion, cut into medium dice

2 carrots, peeled and cut into medium dice (optional)

2 celery stalks, cut into medium dice (optional)

Kosher salt

2 quarts/2 liters chicken stock

8 matzo balls

Chopped gribenes and parsley for garnish (optional)

Make the matzo balls: Combine all the ingredients in a bowl and stir until they are thoroughly mixed. Cover with plastic wrap and set aside at room temperature for 30 minutes, or refrigerate for up to 24 hours.

With damp hands, form the matzo mixture into 8 golf ball–sized orbs (they'll double in size).

Classic Chicken Soup with Matzo Balls
(aka Mr. Fluffies)

Make the soup: In a large pot, melt the schmaltz over high heat, add the onion (and carrots and celery, if using), and cook for a few minutes, just until the onion is translucent, giving it a four-finger pinch of salt as you stir.

Add the stock and bring it to a simmer. Taste it and add more salt, if necessary. Add the matzo balls and let the soup return to a simmer. Reduce the heat to low, cover the pot, and simmer until the matzo balls are cooked through, 20 to 30 minutes. Garnish with gribenes and parsley, if using.

Serves 8.

Traditional Chopped Liver

Until I began working on this book, I had never made chopped liver, and I couldn't tell you the last time I'd tasted it. I'd had plenty of French pâtés that used liver, but not chopped liver like you'd find in a good deli. This is one such recipe. It's great as is, spread on toast or crackers as a snack. Or you can turn this into an elegant hors d'oeuvre, garnished with gribenes and chives, every bit as fine as a French country pâté (see *Pâté de Foie Gras en Terrine*, page 107).

Traditional Chopped Liver

Your grandma, if she made chopped liver, might actually have chopped it all so that it was coarse and chunky. I recommend this, especially if you have a *hoch-messer* (a mezzaluna-shaped knife) and a wooden bowl, which was traditionally how it was done. But chopping with a chef's knife works well, too. Lois, on the other hand, passes her ingredients through a meat grinder, which results in a uniform paste. I like that everything is ground for a smooth, spreadable consistency. A food processor will also work; in fact, if you want to leave some chunks, you can control the texture with a processor in a way you can't with a grinder.

Schmaltz is used to cook the onions and liver, but it's also stirred in at the end to flavor and "moisten" the mixture—it actually has the effect of lightening the pâté. Season aggressively with salt and pepper because it will be eaten cold or at room temperature and so needs the additional salt. Lois notes that it's important to grind and mix the ingredients while they're warm so that the schmaltz is easily absorbed into the mixture until it all becomes very smooth.

I've taken Lois's basic version and added more pepper and also red wine vinegar, to heighten the flavor and balance the richness, which Lois finds bizarre. Taste for yourself; if you want to make Lois's version, simply omit the vinegar and gribenes.

This can be served any way you wish—spread on water crackers, on matzo, on rye toast. It's wonderfully rich, so a little bit goes a long way. Something tart, such as dill pickles or pickled red onions, would make a great counterpoint as an additional garnish. Or, per Lois's recommendation, use it as a component in a corned beef on rye sandwich—fabulous!

Traditional Chopped Liver

3 large eggs

¾ cup/180 grams schmaltz, or more to taste

1 Spanish onion, thinly sliced

1 pound/450 grams chicken livers

1 teaspoon kosher salt, plus more for sautéing the liver

1 teaspoon freshly ground black pepper

2 teaspoons red wine vinegar (optional)

Gribenes (optional)

In a small saucepan, cover the eggs with 1 inch/3 centimeters of water, and bring the water to a boil over high heat. As soon as the water reaches a full boil, cover the pan and take it off the heat. Let the eggs sit in the covered pan, off the heat, for 12 to 15 minutes, then remove them from the water.

Meanwhile, in a large sauté pan over medium heat, melt a third of the schmaltz, and cook the onion in it until it's completely tender and on the brink of browning, 10 to 15 minutes. Transfer the cooked onion to a plate.

Traditional Chopped Liver

Add a little more schmaltz to the pan, increase the heat to high, and sauté the livers, salting them as you do, until they are warm all through with just some pinkness remaining, 7 to 10 minutes.

Peel the eggs. Run all the ingredients through a meat grinder fitted with a small die into a mixing bowl. Add 1 teaspoon salt, the pepper, and the vinegar, if using, and stir to combine. Stir in ½ cup/120 milliliters of the schmaltz, in addition to the gribenes, if using (you can also wait and sprinkle them on top as a garnish), and continue to stir until all the ingredients are well incorporated. (As noted, this can also be done using a food processor.) Taste it and add more schmaltz, salt, vinegar, and pepper as you wish. Chill completely.

Yield: about 2 cups/600 grams

Egg and Gribenes Spread

Egg and Gribenes Spread

I wanted to include this Baron family recipe because it underscores how rooted in poverty Jewish cuisine is. This is a traditional spread to be served on crackers or toast, an easy and inexpensive canapé. It shows off the versatility of the egg, the power of schmaltz to enrich, the forcefulness of the gribenes to flavor, and the power of the onion. Onion and egg, that's it. In its plainest form—egg, sautéed onion, gribenes, schmaltz, salt, and pepper—it's good but very plain. Arthur Schwartz's version, chopped by hand and mashed slightly with a fork, is even plainer—eggs, schmaltz, salt, and pepper, enlivened with raw onion. That said, its greatness lies in this simplicity.

Lois is going to get a little huffy, but I've fallen back on my habit of giving this a little sparkle with some minced shallot macerated in lemon, a kick with cayenne, a little more depth of flavor with fish sauce, and a nice crunch from some diced celery folded in—but it's up to you. No matter how you make it, it goes great on water crackers, matzo, or thinly sliced toast, and would be a great garnish for a green, leafy salad. For a more fanciful canapé, combine it with chopped liver.

This recipe can be doubled.

Egg and Gribenes Spread

4 large eggs

½ Spanish onion, finely diced

1 to 2 tablespoons/15 to 30 grams schmaltz

Kosher salt

Freshly ground black pepper

2 tablespoons/15 grams gribenes

Optional additions, with apologies to Lois:

¼ teaspoon cayenne

1 tablespoon minced shallot macerated in 1 tablespoon lemon juice for at least 5 minutes

1 teaspoon fish sauce

1 small celery stalk, diced

In a small saucepan, cover the eggs with 1 inch/3 centimeters of water and bring the water to a boil over high heat. As soon as the water reaches a full boil, cover the pan and take it off the heat. Let the eggs sit in the covered pan, off the heat, for 12 to 15 minutes, then remove them from the water. (Or, if you have a pressure

Egg and Gribenes Spread

cooker, steam them for 7 minutes, then chill; these are invariably easier to peel.) Run the eggs under cold water, or transfer them to an ice bath, till they're thoroughly chilled. Peel the eggs.

Meanwhile, in a separate small saucepan over medium heat, sauté half the onion in 1 teaspoon schmaltz till translucent. It's a good idea to give it a pinch of salt as you do this, so don't be shy. Transfer the onion to a plate and allow to cool slightly.

Combine all the ingredients except the celery, if using, and gribenes and do any of the following: put them through a meat grinder fitted with a medium or small die; coarsely chop them in a food processor; chop by hand and finish by mashing to a pleasing consistency with a fork. Then fold in the celery, if using, and the gribenes.

Yield: 2 cups/350 grams

Potato Kugel

This is simply hash browns given amazing flavor and crispness from the schmaltz. Potato kugel is no different from latkes, except that schmaltz is added to the mixture here, whereas latkes are shaped into patties and then fried in schmaltz. (Potato kugel is considerably different from noodle kugel, which uses cheese and more eggs and is sweetened with sugar and spices.) The eggs allow you to call this a kugel, but it's basically just a giant latke—every bit as tasty, twice as easy, and the cook can sit down with everyone else and eat it hot.

Potato Kugel

I shred potatoes by hand on a box grater because it's faster than cleaning up the food processor, but feel free to use a processor fitted with the shredder blade.

I like to cook this kugel in a 12-inch/30-centimeter cast-iron skillet because it's so convenient and makes a great serving vessel, but a baking dish will work perfectly fine. Leftovers can be reheated in a toaster oven; try serving leftovers with a poached egg on top!

Potato Kugel

1 large Spanish onion	1½ teaspoons freshly ground black pepper
3 large russet potatoes, peeled and submerged in cold water	2 large eggs, beaten
½ cup/120 grams schmaltz	2 tablespoons/15 grams matzo meal
1½ teaspoons kosher salt	

Preheat the oven to 400°F/200°C.

Grate the onion on the medium holes of a box grater. With your hands, squeeze out as much liquid as possible and put the onion in a large bowl. Grate the potatoes. After each potato, put the shreds in a kitchen towel and squeeze out as much liquid as possible, then toss it with the onion to prevent it from turning brown.

Grease a large skillet or baking dish with a little schmaltz. Add the remaining schmaltz to the potato mixture and toss well.

Add the salt and pepper to the eggs and beat them some more to distribute the seasoning. Add the eggs to the potatoes and onion and toss to thoroughly mix everything. Add the matzo meal and mix to incorporate. Transfer the mixture to the skillet or baking dish and smooth out the surface to make it level.

Potato Kugel

Bake the kugel until it's cooked through and golden brown and crisp on top, about 1 hour. This can be completed a half hour before you want to serve it and then reheated in the oven for 10 minutes before serving.

Serves 6 to 8.

The Mighty Knish

When I moved to New York City in 1985 to take a job as a copyboy at the *New York Times*, I lived at 39th Street and First Avenue, near enough to walk to the Times building, then on 43rd Street in Times Square. Often I would stop at a street vendor and buy a knish for a buck or two. They were crisp on the outside and soft and potatoey on the inside; with some New York City mustard they were deeply satisfying and often served as lunch on my way in to work.

The Mighty Knish

I had no idea that knishes had an actual history. America was just coming out of the culinary dark ages—I was a twenty-two-year-old boy from Cleveland who didn't even know that fresh basil existed. But of course knishes have a history that is glorious for its simplicity and necessity: mashed potatoes baked in dough, all enriched with schmaltz. Potatoes *en croûte*.

Because it's starch in starch, it's important that each one be done with care. The mashed potatoes should be well seasoned and deeply flavored from the fat and gribenes and onion—creamy, not gluey, with a light, flaky crust.

Arthur Schwartz has written several pages on the origins of the knish (the potato version seems to have been invented in New York City) and the derivation of the name (from the word dumpling); he suggests that they were originally filled with meat in Europe. Karen Wise, who copyedited this book, grew up on meat-filled knishes at home in Boston. But the potato and kasha (buckwheat groats) versions seem to be the predominant forms here.*

*Lois gave me a kasha recipe, and also made me a kasha-filled knish, for which I was grateful, but I find kasha appalling and so am not including it in this book. Lois told me that her husband, Russell, leaves the house every time she makes it. I'd say Russell knows what he's doing.

The Mighty Knish

Most important to me is that knishes are apparently dangerous. In the 1990s, Mayor Giuliani had them banned from street carts. All the more reason to make them yourself, I say.

There are different styles of knishes, depending on how they're wrapped and how they're cooked. The kind that I remember, the ones Czar Rudy banned, had a thick crust and were deep-fried. These, according to Schwartz, were created in 1921 by Elia and Bella Gabay; their company, Gabila & Sons Knishes, today makes 1.5 million knishes a year. But traditionally, knishes are baked, and this is how Lois does them. If you use plenty of schmaltz, this is a good strategy.

An important note: Part of the success of the knish lies in rolling out the dough very thinly. I have yet to make my dough thin enough to please Lois, who herself has a love-hate relationship with flour. She insists that the dough must be rolled so thin as to be translucent. To do this and still be able to roll the knishes, Lois recommends that you use a floured pastry cloth, which not only prevents dough from sticking to your work surface but also allows you to lift the delicate dough over the potato filling (and I concur).

The Mighty Knish

DOUGH:

3 to 3½ cups/450 grams all-purpose flour

2 teaspoons baking powder

½ cup/120 grams schmaltz, well chilled (you can use vegetable oil if you wish)

½ cup/120 milliliters water

1 large egg

1 teaspoon kosher salt

½ teaspoon freshly ground black pepper (optional)

FILLING:

⅓ cup/80 grams schmaltz, or more to taste

2 Spanish onions, finely diced

2 to 3 teaspoons kosher salt, or more to taste

3 large russet potatoes (about 3 pounds/1.4 kilograms), peeled and cut into 6 to 8 pieces each *or* 4 cups/750 grams plain mashed or riced potatoes

¼ cup/30 grams gribenes (optional)

1 teaspoon freshly ground black pepper, or more to taste

1 large egg, beaten

1 large egg whisked with 1 tablespoon water

Make the dough: Combine the flour, baking powder, and chilled schmaltz in the bowl of a standing mixer fitted with the paddle attachment and mix on medium-high speed until the fat is uniformly mixed into the flour. Stop the mixer and replace the paddle with the dough hook. Add the water, egg, salt, and pepper (if using) and mix till the dough comes together, another minute or two. Shape the dough into a rectangle about 2 inches/5 centimeters thick, wrap in plastic, and refrigerate for at least 1 hour or up to 24 hours.

The Mighty Knish

Make the filling: Melt ¼ cup/60 grams schmaltz in a large pot or Dutch oven over high heat. Add the onions, hit them with 1 teaspoon salt, and stir to coat them. Reduce the heat to low and let them cook, stirring occasionally, until they're lightly browned, 1 to 1½ hours.

Meanwhile, if you're starting with raw potatoes, cover them with water and simmer till they're completely tender, but not disintegrating, 20 to 30 minutes. Mash them by hand or pass them through a ricer or food mill. Set aside while the onions cook. The potatoes can be covered and refrigerated for up to a day, so this step can be done in advance. So can the onions, for that matter.

When the onions are nicely browned, add the potatoes, the gribenes (if using), another teaspoon of salt, and the pepper and stir to combine. Add a couple more tablespoons of schmaltz (don't be stingy!). Taste and add more salt and pepper as needed. Remove from the heat and stir in the beaten egg. Transfer the potato filling to a bowl, cover, and refrigerate until you're ready to make the knishes—it will keep for up to 2 days.

Make the knishes: Preheat the oven to 400°F/200°C.

Cut your chilled dough into three rectangles. Refrigerate two while you roll out the first one. Roll it out as thin as possible, preferably on a floured pastry cloth, into a rectangle 6 to 8 inches/15 to 20 centimeters wide and about twice as long. Trim the edges with a knife, pastry wheel, or pizza cutter so that you have a uniform rectangle. (Save the trimmings if you want, to make additional knishes.)

The Mighty Knish

Using one-third of the potato filling, form a log about 1½ inches/4 centimeters in diameter. Place the log along one long edge of the dough rectangle, leaving 1 inch/3 centimeters space at either short end. Roll the dough over the potato filling and keep rolling till you have a neat tube, with the seam side down.

Using the edge of your hand, press down on the dough in gentle karate chop fashion, to form 3-inch/8-centimeter knishes. Be gentle but firm. Slice through the dough with a knife to separate the knishes and pinch their edges shut. Put them on a baking sheet and brush them with the egg wash. Repeat with the remaining dough rectangles and potato filling. Bake for 15 to 20 minutes.

Serve immediately. Or, if you want to serve the knishes later in the day, leave them at room temperature and then reheat them in the oven. Store cooled knishes in an airtight container or well wrapped in plastic in the refrigerator for 3 to 4 days or in the freezer for up to 3 weeks.

Yield: about 20 knishes

1. Roll out the dough as thin as possible, preferably on a pastry cloth, which helps with both the rolling and the shaping. →

2. The dough should be thin and supple. →

3. Cut the dough into large rectangles and shape the filling into cylinders the length of the dough. Brush the far end of the dough with egg wash to ensure a good seal. →

4. Roll the dough over the filling. →

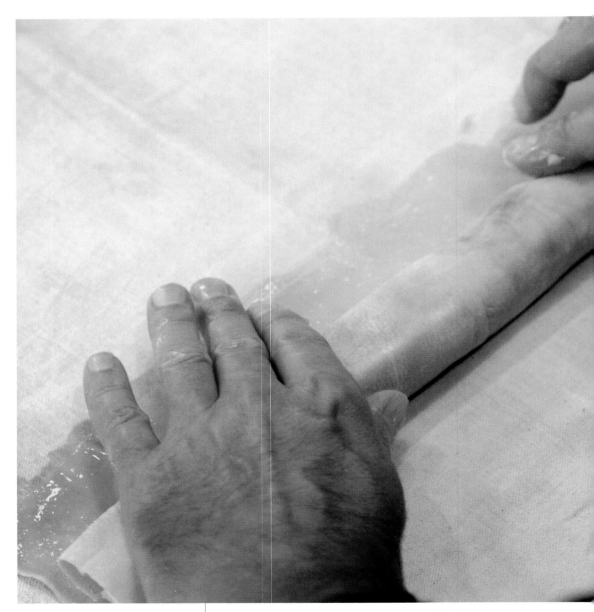

5. Continue rolling the dough over the filling to form a cylinder. →

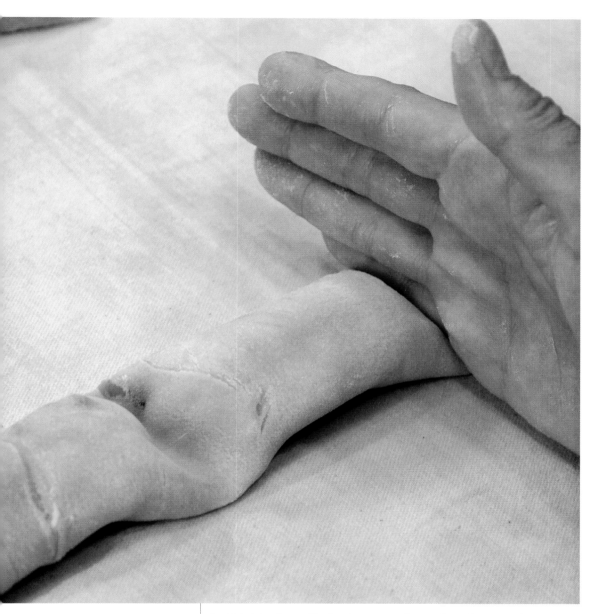

6. Divide the cylinder into equal portions by pressing down on it with the side of your hand. This will help seal the edges of the dough and prevent the filling from falling out.　　　→

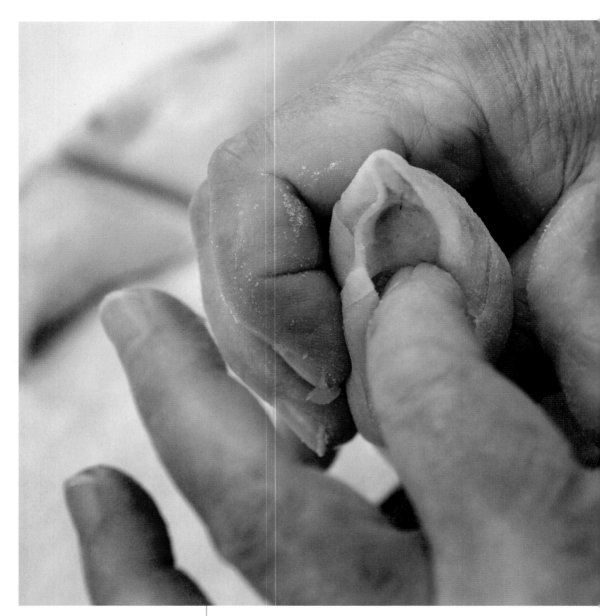

7. Cut the individual knishes apart and press any loose filling at the ends back into the knish. →

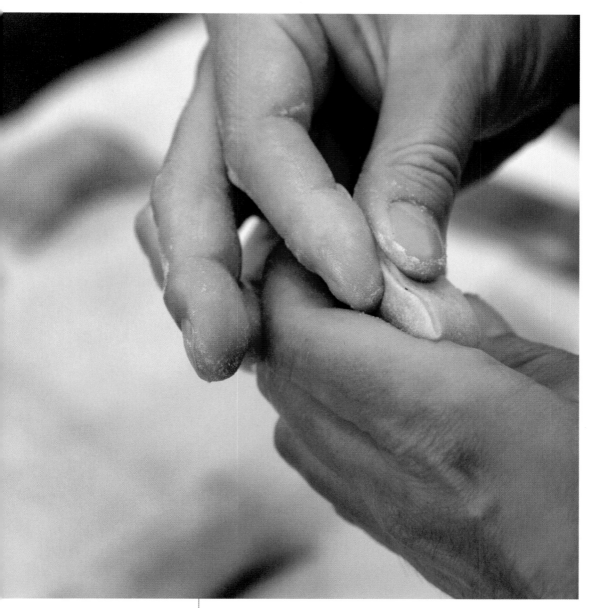

8. Pinch the knish ends together to seal them.   →

9. Place the knishes on a parchment-lined baking sheet and brush each knish with egg wash. Bake till golden brown.

Kreplach

Kreplach are dumplings filled with cooked ground meat. Most recipes call for braising a brisket specifically for this purpose, but it would not be unreasonable to presume that kreplach originated as a way to use leftover meat. It is fabulous for that. The reason anyone would suggest that you braise meat specifically for

Kreplach

kreplach is easy to fathom: Kreplach are better than beef brisket. They are traditionally served in soup, but I know for a fact that they are outstanding sautéed in schmaltz till crisp, not only for the flavor but also for the crunchy chewiness of the dough when browned.

Researching kreplach, I had a look at Arthur Schwartz's recipe and saw that his dough is almost exactly the same as Lois's version here. Lois found this interesting but not surprising. Her recipe comes from a little white piece of paper with tattered edges, written by her mother, and dated 1935. "Maybe it was a celebratory dinner—that was the year I was born," Lois said. On further thought, she noted that recipes were typically passed from family to family, and the ones that worked best likely spread farthest. Schwartz didn't make his up. He got it from Cindy Klotz in New York, who got it from her grandmother. Who knows, maybe that very recipe spread all the way to Cleveland, or vice versa.

In any case, it's a fabulous dough—very pliable, workable, and easy to roll out without too much sticking. Try to roll it out as thin as possible—it expands quite a bit when boiled.

I like to serve these fried, with braised cabbage, the recipe for which follows. But feel free to use kreplach any way you wish—whether in soup or on a bed of sautéed onions with sour cream, they're excellent.

Kreplach

DOUGH:

2 large eggs, beaten

¼ cup/60 milliliters water

2 cups/280 grams all-purpose flour

FILLING:

1 large egg, beaten

1 pound/455 grams cooked beef (preferably leftover beef brisket)

½ Spanish onion, diced, sautéed in schmaltz till tender, cooled

2 cloves garlic, smashed or minced to a paste

¼ cup/60 grams schmaltz

1½ teaspoons freshly ground black pepper

1 tablespoon sweet Hungarian paprika

1 large egg, whisked with 1 tablespoon/15 milliliters water

¼ cup/60 grams schmaltz

Make the dough: Combine all the ingredients in the bowl of a standing mixer fitted with the paddle attachment and mix on medium-high speed until the dough is baby's-bottom smooth. You may want to remove the dough from the bowl and finish kneading it by hand, which is fun. (Indeed, the dough can be made start to finish by hand if you don't have a stand mixer.) Wrap the dough in plastic while you make the filling. The dough should be left at room temperature if you're making the kreplach that day, or it can be refrigerated for up to a day.

Kreplach

Make the filling: Combine the first seven ingredients and pass through a meat grinder fitted with a small die, then stir well or purée in a food processor until it's all uniformly combined.

Make the kreplach: Roll out the dough as thin as possible, less than ⅛ inch/ 3 millimeters thick, using a rolling pin or a pasta roller. Cut the dough into 3-inch/ 8.5-centimeter squares (it helps to use a ruler to guide your cutting). Spoon 1 teaspoon filling into the center of each square. Brush two adjacent sides of each square with the egg wash and fold the dough over the filling, sealing the filling in and creating a triangle-shaped kreplach.

Bring a large pot of water to a boil. Boil the kreplach until the dough is cooked, 3 to 5 minutes. Drain the kreplach in a colander and run cold water over them until chilled. Toss the kreplach with a little vegetable oil to prevent them from sticking together. At this point, the kreplach can be stored in a plastic bag or container for up to 3 days in the refrigerator or up to a month in the freezer.

To fry the kreplach after boiling them, heat the schmaltz in a large sauté pan over medium-high heat. Fry the kreplach until golden brown, a couple minutes on each side. (If you've frozen them, allow them to thaw before frying, of course.)

The kreplach can also be added to beef or chicken stock for great soup dumplings.

Yield: about 40 kreplach

To serve the kreplach on braised cabbage:

2 tablespoons/30 grams schmaltz or other fat or vegetable oil

4 cups/500 grams shredded cabbage

½ Spanish onion, cut into medium dice

1 cup/240 milliliters chicken stock

3 tablespoons whole-grain mustard

Kosher salt and freshly ground black pepper

Red wine vinegar to taste

In a large sauté pan over high heat, melt 1 tablespoon/15 grams schmaltz. Just before it begins to smoke, add the cabbage and onion. Spread the vegetables evenly over the pan and leave them alone a minute or two to brown. Lower the heat to medium, toss the vegetables, and continue cooking till the cabbage wilts, 5 more minutes. Add the chicken stock and bring to a simmer, then reduce the heat to low. Stir in the mustard, and season with salt, pepper, and red wine vinegar to taste. Serve when the stock has reduced by three-quarters and the ingredients are uniformly combined.

To serve, place the kreplach on a bed of sautéed cabbage and serve as you wish— with more mustard, sour cream, and a pinch of cayenne.

1. A simple egg-and-water pasta dough is rolled out and cut into uniform squares, ready to receive a heaping teaspoon of the filling. →

2. Egg wash will help seal the dumplings. →

3. Fold corner to corner, pressing the filling into the center of the dough. →

4. Strain chicken stock directly into the sautéed cabbage. →

5. The dumplings can be frozen before or after boiling them. They can be reheated in water, added to soups, or sautéed until browned and crisp—preferably in more schmaltz! →

6. Kreplach don't get the nickname Jewish potstickers for nothing. →

7. To plate the dish, make a bed of the cabbage.

Kishke

Kishke is a starch-based stuffing that was once served at every Jewish celebration but has fallen out of fashion, according to Arthur Schwartz. It's simple to make and delicious, and deserves to be resurrected. The word *kishke* is Yiddish for "gut," because the filling was traditionally stuffed into a cow intestine casing—or, in the case of helzel, into a chicken or goose neck (some refer to it as "stuffed derma," or skin). Schwartz notes that the starch used in the stuffing could be anything—potato, flour, matzo meal, barley, or crackers (Joan Nathan's choice).

Kishke

Kishke's rich flavor and ease of preparation are reasons enough to return it to the table. It's a delicious and satisfying side dish. Schwartz uses raw vegetables in his kishke, but I prefer Lois's version, which gets a boost of deep flavor from cooking the vegetables in schmaltz. The vegetables and remaining ingredients are then puréed in a food processor. Lois wraps hers in a parchment cylinder (Schwartz and Nathan use foil) and roasts it. It can then be sliced and served or, better, sliced and sautéed in schmaltz (or vegetable oil) to crisp it up.

Given all my experience with my books *Charcuterie* and *Salumi*, though, I see no reason not to go old-school and stuff it into beef middles (available by mail or from a kosher butcher). It can then be cooked along with a brisket, for instance (see my Cholent, page 81, where it is a component). A few pointers: Stuff it very loosely, about half the diameter of the casing, because it will expand; tie very tight knots in the ends, which are slippery; and poke several holes in the casing to let expanding air and steam out or it will burst.

Notice that there's no liquid added to the kishke, so it's a very dense, moldable, dry paste before it's cooked. That's why kishke must be served with either a gravy or the braising liquid from, say, a pot roast or cholent. I sometimes like to cook kishke in rich chicken or turkey stock, then thicken the stock to make a gravy. Lois likes to make a helzel, though a more contemporary one, stuffed in the skin of a chicken, and I love this, too. In any case, kishke is a delicious and uncommon side dish appropriate for any juicy or gravy-rich main course.

Kishke

What follows is the basic, all-purpose kishke recipe. Traditional kishke doesn't include eggs, and if you're planning to wrap and roast it, there's no need for the eggs included here. I've included them for those who will be cooking the kishke in a casing in liquid, for the eggs' binding properties. Sometimes the casing, when cooked over a long period, becomes so delicate it breaks; the egg will help the kishke maintain its shape in the liquid.

Kishke

½ cup/120 grams schmaltz

1 Spanish onion, cut into large dice

5 garlic cloves, smashed with the flat side of a knife

1 large carrot, peeled and cut into large dice

2 large celery stalks, cut into large dice

1½ teaspoons kosher salt

1½ cups/210 grams matzo meal (or 6 squares of matzo, well pulverized in a food processor)

1½ teaspoons freshly ground black pepper

1 teaspoon sweet Hungarian paprika

2 large eggs, beaten (if using beef casing)

30 inches/75 centimeters beef casing, cut in half and well soaked (optional)

¼ cup/60 milliliters chicken stock

Kishke

Heat ¼ cup/60 grams schmaltz in a large sauté pan over medium-high heat and add the onion, garlic, carrot, celery, and 1 teaspoon salt. Cook it all for a few minutes, stirring, then reduce the heat to medium-low and cook until the vegetables are tender and beginning to brown, another 30 minutes or so. Transfer the vegetables to a plate to cool.

In a food processor, combine the remaining ½ teaspoon salt, matzo meal, pepper, and paprika. Pulse the blade a few times to distribute the seasoning. Add the cooled vegetables, the remaining ¼ cup/60 grams schmaltz, and the eggs, if using. Process until it's uniformly combined; it should hold together when squeezed. If it's too dry, add another few tablespoons of schmaltz or ¼ cup chicken stock and purée some more.

If roasting, preheat the oven to 350°F/180°C.

Divide the kishke onto two sheets of parchment paper or foil, and use your hands to roll it into two 8-inch/21-centimeter cylinders, then wrap in the parchment or foil, twisting the ends to tighten. Place the rolls on a baking sheet and roast for 45 minutes. If serving right away, allow the kishke to cool for 20 minutes before unwrapping and slicing. Otherwise, refrigerate the wrapped kishke till you're ready to reheat (in the microwave or oven, or by slicing and frying).

If you're using beef casing, make sure the casing has been well soaked and flushed with plenty of cold water. Stuff each piece with the kishke by hand; the kishke will double in size, so stuff the casing extremely loosely, only about half the diameter of what the casing will contain. Tie off each end with a strong knot of kitchen

Kishke

string. Poke the casing all over with a knife tip, needle, or sausage pricker to help prevent the casing from bursting—it may burst anyway depending on how you cook it; the casing becomes very delicate, so be gentle.

Poach the kishke in poultry stock at just below a simmer until cooked through, about 30 minutes (don't worry, you can't overcook it). Or, if you prefer, place the kishke in an oven-safe casserole dish, cover with simmering hot stock, and place in a 200°F/95°C oven for 45 minutes.

Serves 6 to 8 as a side dish.

Helzel

This is a dramatic and tasty way to prepare and serve kishke, wrapped in chicken skin with wings still attached and roasted to a golden brown. It would be a great accompaniment for chicken soup made from the carcass and meat, or a perfect side dish for a chicken stew or a braise. And it's an impressive item to serve on a buffet because it's so visually interesting. Be sure to include the eggs when preparing the kishke; this will facilitate binding so that it slices cleanly.

While I'll describe the technique of preparing the skin for this helzel preparation, photos are most helpful, and I recommend you look at those first.

Helzel

One 4-pound/1.8-kilogram chicken

1 recipe Kishke, prepared with eggs

Kosher salt

1 to 2 tablespoons/15 to 30 grams schmaltz

Preheat the oven to 425°F/220°C.

Place the chicken on its back with the drumsticks pointing at you. To remove the leg-thigh pieces, slice through the skin between the leg and breast. Bend the leg-thigh toward you to pop the joint, then finish cutting through the joint and skin that holds the leg to the carcass. You can remove the wing tips so that they can be used in stock, or they can be left on and tucked under the neck area; leaving them on allows for a better presentation (both are pictured).

Begin removing the skin, intact, by starting at the top tip of the breast, lifting it with your fingers and slicing the connective tissue that attaches it to the keel bone separating the breast halves. Continue delicately slicing to remove the skin,

Helzel

but do not cut through the skin or the meat. When the skin is completely off the breast but still attached to the wings, feel for the joint where the wing attaches to the carcass. Slice through the wing joint, taking care not to cut any skin, and then through the meat to separate the wing from the carcass, leaving all the skin still attached to the wing. Do the same with the other wing. The only part of the skin-wing piece still attached to the carcass will be the narrow strip of skin along the back of the bird. Turn the carcass over and slice this skin off the back, and you should be able to remove the skin with wings attached, leaving the carcass with breast meat still attached.

Remove each breast half by slicing along both sides of the keel bone, following the ribs with your knife to remove the breast, leaving as little meat on the ribs as possible. Reserve the legs for another use, as well as the breast halves (perhaps to sauté and serve with Sauce Baron, page 136); save the carcass to make stock for gravy to serve with the helzel.

Place the prepared skin on your cutting board in the same position it was when you began—breast skin on top, back skin on the bottom, wings on either side. Form the kishke into a fat cylinder that will comfortably fit within the skin and place it where the carcass had been. Fold the skin that had covered the backbone over the top of the kishke you've just laid down. Fold the breast skin down around the kishke so that the kishke is entirely enclosed in the skin. Turn the helzel over so that the breast skin is down and you are looking at the back. Using 3 to 5 pieces of butcher's string, secure the skin around the kishke and tie the string snugly but not too tightly around the skin (this will help to keep the skin in place as the

Helzel

helzel roasts). When you've made as many ties as necessary, turn the bird over—breast-side up, knots-side down. Pull the neck skin pieces together and tuck them underneath. Fold the wing tips back underneath the bird if you've left them on. Salt the skin liberally with kosher salt so that it will have a nice salty crust. Place the helzel in a skillet and put it in the oven. After 20 minutes, add a tablespoon or two of schmaltz or butter to the pan, if you wish, and baste the skin to help it brown and cook uniformly. Continue to roast the helzel until the skin is golden brown, another 10 or 20 minutes.

Allow the helzel to rest for 5 or 10 minutes, carefully remove the string (it will be stuck to the bottom), and cut the helzel in ½-inch/1.25-centimeter slices. Whoever prepared the helzel gets at least one of the wings!

Serves 6 to 8 as a side dish.

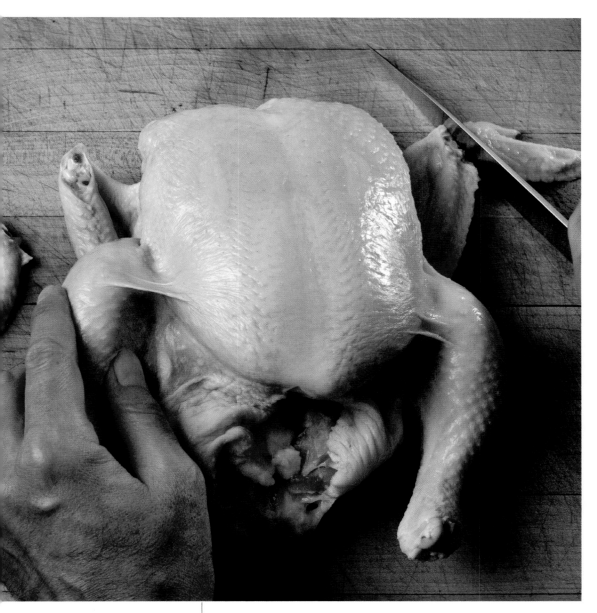

1. To prepare the skin, you'll be removing the legs to use the skin covering the breast and back; an optional step is to remove the wing tips to use for soup or stock. →

2. Remove the legs by slicing through the skin between the leg and the breast.

3. Bend the leg toward you to pop the joint, then cut through the remaining skin and muscle to separate the leg from the carcass (reserve the legs for another use).

4. Reserve the extra fat for more schmaltz!

5. Lift the skin at the tip of the breast, slicing the membrane that attaches it to the keel bone, being careful to keep the skin intact. →

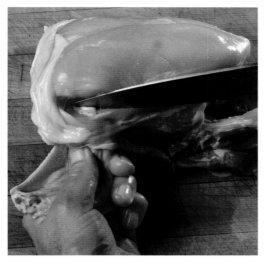

6. Locate the joint where the wing attaches to the carcass.

7. Cut through the joint without cutting through the skin so that the wing remains attached to the skin rather than to the carcass.

8. Continue to remove the skin from the breast.

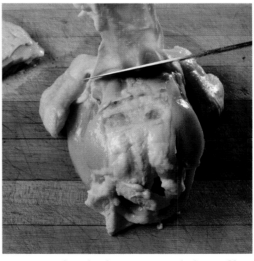

9. Turn the chicken over and slice off the skin attached to the backbone. →

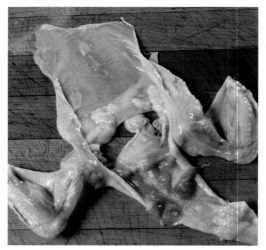

10. You should be left with one intact piece of skin, wings still attached; remove the breast halves from the carcass and reserve them for another use. Use the carcass to make stock.

11. Shape the kishke so that it will fit snugly within the skin.

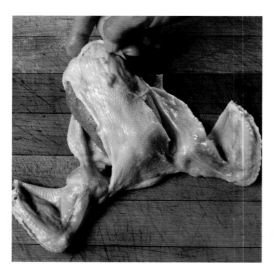

12. Wrap the skin around the kishke.

13. Flip the helzel over and make sure it's nicely formed. You can secure it with string to ensure that the skin remains snug around the kishke and doesn't shrink. It's ready to roast.

Cholent

Of all the dishes in the book, this was the one that I feared most at first and then became most excited about. Every time I even said "cholent," Lois would groan and roll her eyes (apparently there were more cholents in her childhood than she cares to remember). Cholent is the name of a large pot into which a variety of meats and vegetables can be cooked low and slow, started before sundown on Friday and eaten as the Sabbath lunch (no labor whatsoever, certainly not cooking, can be performed from sundown to sundown by observant Jews). My two Jewish

Cholent

food gurus both note its primacy in traditional Jewish cookery. Arthur Schwartz writes that some scholars argue that cholent "is one of only three truly Jewish dishes" (the others, he notes, being matzo and charoset, a sweet and spicy paste of fruits and nuts served during the Passover seder). Joan Nathan likewise notes that cholent "is one of those dishes that has always distinguished Jewish cooking since at least the fourth century A.D." (I'm proud to note that the cholent in Nathan's book *Jewish Cooking in America* comes from a Clevelander, Sara Brizdle Dickman, who suggests that possibilities for cholent were so diverse there ought to be a cholent cook-off in the same way we have a rib cook-off every summer.)

Given its iconic status and Lois's knee-jerk *ugh* reaction, I thought, *Why can't a cholent be fabulous?* It's hardly different from cassoulet, the great French country stew featuring duck and pork. It was with this goal that I set out to devise a cholent that would not only satisfy observant Jews and adhere to Sabbath ritual, but would also be a great dish any day of the week for all—a dish that could be started on, say, a Sunday afternoon (with a football game in the background) to be cooked overnight for a quickly finished Monday night meal for the family. Or simply refrigerated for up to a week and reheated when needed.

Thus my excitement grew. Goose or duck confit was sometimes included in the cholent recipes I consulted (in the fashion of cassoulet), but I like to feature confit crisp and hot if I've gone to the trouble of making it, rather than stew it to death. So for this, the meat is beef short ribs (though beef cheeks are preferable if you can find them, and flanken could be substituted—the recipe below is for 6 serv-

Cholent

ings; if substituting meat, figure on ½ pound/225 grams of bone-in meat or 4 to 6 ounces/120 to 180 grams boneless meat per person).

I wanted the liquid to be water, in keeping with tradition and economy, so I've included veal breast and its bones for flavor and body. Also for flavor, as well as color, tomato paste. I add fish sauce for additional savory depth (certainly Sephardic tradition might well have included anchovy for seasoning), in addition to salt, pepper, and paprika.

Harkening to my love of cassoulet, I recommend Tarbais beans, but any dried legumes will do, soaked overnight (otherwise they may soak up too much of the cooking liquid). I choose potatoes for the starch. Often barley was added; this seems like overkill to me, but feel free to add a cup of barley if you love barley. Some versions call for putting whole eggs in the stew, but this is a waste of good eggs, which turn brown and nasty when cooked for many, many hours. But, again, there's no harm in adding eggs if you like your cholent that way.

If your family is observant of the Sabbath, begin this by midday on Friday; if you follow the recipe exactly, I volunteer to be your House Goy to take it out of the oven (and make fresh gremolata, which is a superb finishing garnish for most braises). If you are simply making this as a great winter meal, there are a number of different ways to cook and finish this dish, which I'll outline below.

Cholent

CHOLENT:

One 4-pound/1.8-kilogram breast of veal

6 to 8 meaty beef short ribs (boneless short ribs, beef cheeks, or flanken can be substituted as desired; see headnote for quantities)

Kosher salt

All-purpose flour for dredging

Schmaltz or vegetable oil as needed

1½ cups/250 grams Tarbais beans, navy beans, or a mix of dried beans, soaked overnight (see note below if you forget to soak)

½ recipe Kishke (page 67), prepared in a 15-inch/40-centimeter beef casing (optional)

2 russet potatoes, peeled and quartered

1 Spanish onion, peeled and quartered, with the root end still attached so the layers stay together

3 carrots, peeled

3 celery stalks

3 bay leaves

¼ cup/70 grams tomato paste

2 teaspoons freshly ground black pepper

2 teaspoons paprika (optional)

GREMOLATA:

¼ cup/30 grams finely chopped flat-leaf parsley

1 tablespoon/15 grams finely minced garlic

1 tablespoon/15 grams grated lemon zest

Preheat the oven to 450°F/230°C (or 425°F/220°C if you're worried about smoke).

Separate the veal ribs, then slice them in half crosswise where the bone ends and the cartilage begins. Put the ribs on a sheet pan and roast them until they're golden brown and smell delicious, 30 to 40 minutes. Reserve any rendered fat.

Cholent

Reduce the oven temperature as low as it will go—180°F/82°C is ideal, but 200°F/95°C is fine, too.

Give the short ribs a liberal sprinkling of salt and dredge them in flour. In a large, heavy-gauge sauté pan, cast-iron skillet, or enameled cast-iron Dutch oven over high heat, sear all sides of the beef ribs in the reserved rendered veal fat, plus additional schmaltz or vegetable oil as needed, a few minutes per side. Remove to a paper towel–lined plate. Both the veal ribs and the beef ribs can be prepared up to 3 days before assembling the cholent for cooking; allow them to cool, cover with plastic wrap, and refrigerate until needed.

Drain the beans from their soaking liquid. (If you forgot to soak them overnight, put them in a pot, cover with 2 inches/5 centimeters of water, bring the water to a boil, remove the pan from the heat, cover, let sit for an hour, and then drain.) Add the beans to a large stockpot, followed by the veal ribs, the short ribs, and the rest of the ingredients. Try to keep the celery and carrot whole, or halved (they and the onion will be discarded after cooking—they can be bound with string for easy removal if you have room). Add enough water (3 to 4 quarts/ 3 to 4 liters) so that the veal and the beans are completely submerged. If using kishke, poke the casing all over with a knife tip, needle, or sausage pricker to help prevent the casing from bursting. Cover the pot and put it in the oven for 12 to 24 hours.

Cholent

Just before you're ready to serve the cholent, combine the gremolata ingredients in a small bowl. Or, make it up to a day ahead of time, cover it with plastic wrap, and refrigerate it.

Discard the onion, carrots, celery, and bay leaves. (You can leave the veal in if you want, but it will have no flavor whatsoever; your dog will appreciate the bones.) To serve immediately, divide the beef and potatoes in each bowl and add a big scoop of beans. Slice the kishke and add a slice to each bowl. Skim the layer of fat that rises to the top of the liquid (this fat is delicious and can be used for further cooking). Ladle the sauce over the meat, potatoes, beans, and kishke and garnish with gremolata.

TO MAKE CHOLENT AHEAD OF TIME TO EAT ON THE SABBATH OR DURING THE WEEK:

Cholent can be cooked, cooled, and refrigerated as is for up to a week before serving. Remove the layer of fat that will congeal on its surface before reheating. Discard the carrot, onion, celery, and veal now if you haven't already, and rewarm the stew on the stovetop. The kishke casing will be extremely delicate at this point, so remove it when just warm. When the liquid is piping hot, serve as described above.

TO MAKE THIS DISH AS A WEEKDAY MEAL:

You have a couple of options. The cholent will be fully cooked in about 6 hours if you put it in a 275°F/135°C oven. If you want to cook it even faster, don't use the

Cholent

veal (there won't be enough time for flavor development and gelatin extraction); bring it all to a simmer on the stovetop, cover it, and put it in a 300°F/150°C oven for 2 to 4 hours.

MY FAVORITE WAY TO SERVE THIS DISH:

If you've cooked the cholent in a low oven overnight, many of the beans will be cracked and fragmented. The stock will be the consistency of clear soup. My favorite way to serve cholent that has cooked for this long is to discard the veal, carrot, celery, onion, and bay leaves, then transfer the beef and potatoes to a bowl and cover with plastic wrap. Drain the beans in a colander placed over a second pot; pour this liquid through a fine-mesh strainer back into the original cooking pot. Skim the fat that rises to the top and discard or reserve it for more cooking. Return the beans to the strained, defatted cooking liquid. Purée the beans in the cooking liquid using a handheld blender (or do it in batches in a standing blender). The result will be a thick, delicious, smooth sauce. Add the beef and potatoes and bring to a simmer, then serve with the gremolata.

Serves 6 with leftovers.

1. Cholent mise en place, clockwise from left: roasted veal bones, seared beef, potatoes, beans, aromatic vegetables, salt, tomato paste, black pepper, bay leaves, and kishke. →

2. Begin layering the stew by putting the beans in first, followed by the veal bones and vegetables that will flavor the water, potatoes, kishke, and remaining ingredients. →

3. Add the kishke last. →

4. Cover the ingredients with water.   →

5. Poke a few holes in the kishke to let steam escape. →

6. The cholent just out of the oven. →

7. For a more refined version, strain the cooking liquid into a large container. Portion out beans, potatoes, beef, and kishke into bowls and pour piping hot sauce over it all.

Contemporary Recipes

Schmaltz is firmly rooted in Jewish cuisine for a reason. Because all things porcine, including the valuable and abundant fat, are forbidden by Jewish dietary law, Jews have long relied on fat from poultry to cook with. But because chicken fat was chosen for religious reasons is no reason to relegate it to a single cuisine. Schmaltz is worth holding up to the light for all to revere and to recognize for what it is: a marvel of flavor, and a fabulous cooking tool that all cooks in all lands should embrace.

For this reason, I've created several dishes for the contemporary kitchen that do not hew to any culinary tradition or religious affiliation, but rather are meant to highlight schmaltz itself. Some are variations on traditional Jewish cuisine; others are completely separate from it. All are delicious because of schmaltz.

Vichyssoise with Gribenes
and Chives (page 98)

Four-Star Matzo Ball Soup
(page 101)

Pâté de Foie Gras en Terrine
with Croutons (page 107)

Schmaltz-Roasted Potatoes with
Onion and Rosemary (page 111)

Chicken with Schmaltz Dumplings 1
(quick and easy, page 115)

Chicken with Schmaltz Dumplings 2
(from scratch, page 117)

Parisienne Gnocchi with Spinach,
Onion, and Poached Egg (page 121)

Chicken Confit
(page 127)

Chicken Rillettes
(page 132)

Chicken *Suprêmes* with Sauce Baron
(page 136)

Chicken Sausage (page 140)

Savory Brioche (page 144)

Scones with Roasted Red Pepper and
Parmigiano-Reggiano (page 148)

Oatmeal Cookies with Dried Cherries
(page 152)

Vichyssoise with Gribenes and Chives

This chilled potato and leek soup is an easy and elegant first course that is ideal when the weather's warm, though it could also be served hot when the weather's cold. The key to its elegance is the texture. The schmaltz flavors the onions, and the gribenes add both textural contrast and flavor to the soup. I like to leave chunks of onion for texture and visual appeal, but the onions and leeks can be sautéed together if you prefer a perfectly smooth soup. Don't overblend the potatoes or the texture can become gummy. You'll need about a tablespoon each of the gribenes and chives per serving.

Vichyssoise with Gribenes and Chives

¼ cup/60 grams schmaltz

½ Spanish onion, cut into medium dice

Kosher salt

1 large leek, white and pale green parts only, cleaned and roughly chopped

1 large russet potato, peeled and cut into large dice

¼ teaspoon cayenne pepper

2 cups/500 milliliters chicken stock, plus more as needed

½ cup/120 milliliters heavy cream

Fresh lemon juice or white wine vinegar to taste

Finely chopped gribenes, for garnish

Finely minced chives, for garnish

Heat 2 tablespoons of the schmaltz in a medium sauté pan over medium-high heat, add the onion and a three-finger pinch of salt, and cook until the onion just begins to brown, about 5 minutes. Transfer the onion to a plate. The onion can be browned up to a day ahead of time, covered, and refrigerated.

Melt the remaining 2 tablespoons schmaltz in the same pan over medium heat. Add the leek and a four-finger pinch of salt. Cook until the leek is tender but not browned, 3 to 5 minutes.

Vichyssoise with Gribenes and Chives

Add the potato and stir to coat with the fat. Add the cayenne and the stock. Raise the heat to bring the stock to a simmer, then reduce the heat to maintain a gentle simmer. Cook until the potatoes are tender, 10 to 15 minutes.

Using a hand blender or a standing blender, purée the soup just long enough so that its texture is uniform, then pass the soup through a fine-mesh strainer.

Taste the soup and add more salt if necessary. This soup will be eaten cold, so you'll need to season it aggressively. Stir in the browned diced onion. Stir in the cream. If the soup is too thick, thin it with some chicken stock. It should be the consistency of heavy cream.

Chill the soup thoroughly. Taste the soup and season it with lemon juice or white wine vinegar as needed. Serve the soup garnished with gribenes and chives.

Serves 4 to 6.

Four-Star Matzo Ball Soup

Don't think of matzo ball soup only as comfort food, to be eaten on a cold Sunday afternoon in pajamas and an old sweater. While it may have originated as a post-Passover way to use up leftover matzo, a matzo ball can make an elegant starting course for a meal, served in smaller bowls to feature a single matzo ball, and well garnished. The parsley is optional here, but it adds color and flavor. You might replace the parsley with tarragon or chives or a mixture of the three.

Four-Star Matzo Ball Soup

Variations are, of course, infinite. I'm going to go all out here and make this very elegant, but with technique rather than ingredients (though black truffle shavings would be an awesome way to finish this soup). Make a garnish of nicely cut vegetables, cook and shock them so they're tender and vividly colored, and finish it with gribenes and freshly chopped parsley. I'm even enhancing the matzo balls with sautéed onion.

Want to put this over the top for an elegant dinner party? One extra step can be done a day or more ahead: Clarify the stock—it's fun and dramatic. Then cook everything separately, even the matzo balls. Keep them hot in a covered pan of stock, then compose the soup in hot bowls, starting with the vegetables and hot matzo ball, and then the consommé, for a beautiful presentation.

Four-Star Matzo Ball Soup

MATZO BALLS:

2 tablespoons/30 grams schmaltz

½ Spanish onion, cut into small dice

Kosher salt

½ cup/70 grams matzo meal (or 2 squares of matzo, well pulverized in a food processor)

2 large eggs, beaten

2 tablespoons/30 milliliters chicken stock or water, plus additional for simmering

½ teaspoon baking powder

¼ teaspoon freshly ground black pepper

SOUP:

1 Spanish onion, cut into small dice

2 celery stalks, cut on the bias into ¼-inch slices

2 carrots, peeled and cut into small dice

Kosher salt to taste

1½ quarts/1.5 liters chicken stock or consommé (recipe follows)

½ cup/60 grams gribenes

¼ cup chopped flat-leaf parsley

Make the matzo balls: Heat the schmaltz in a medium sauté pan over medium-high heat, add the onion and a three-finger pinch of salt, and cook until the onion just begins to brown, about 5 minutes. Transfer the onion and fat to a plate to cool.

Combine the remaining ingredients, along with a four-finger pinch of salt, in a large bowl. Add the cooled onion and fat. Stir the mixture thoroughly until all ingredients are uniformly mixed. Cover with plastic wrap and let sit for at least 30 minutes, or refrigerate for up to 24 hours.

Four-Star Matzo Ball Soup

With damp hands, form the matzo mixture into 4 balls, making them as big, smooth, and round as ping-pong balls. Place them in a saucepan of simmering chicken stock, cover the pan, and cook for 20 minutes. If you're making the soup right away, keep the matzo balls in the stock, covered. If not, allow them to cool, wrap individually in plastic, and refrigerate.

Make the soup: Bring a large pot of water to a boil, and ready an ice bath. When the water boils, add the onion and cook for 30 seconds. Scoop out the onion with a strainer and dip the strainer into the bowl of ice water, stirring the onion till chilled. Put it in a paper towel–lined bowl and cover with plastic wrap. Do the same with the celery. Do the same with the carrot, but cook the carrot for 60 to 90 seconds before removing it to the ice bath.

Bring the stock to a simmer. Taste, and season with salt if necessary. Heat your soup bowls in the oven or in a microwave. Reheat your matzo balls in stock if necessary (if you're serving clarified stock, heat the matzo balls in separate stock or they can cloud the consommé).

Make a bed with the blanched onion in the center of each bowl; ring the carrot around the onion, and the celery around the carrot. Place a hot matzo ball on the onion. Add the piping hot stock or consommé to the bowl. Pouring the stock into the prepared bowls is especially dramatic to do at the table if you've taken the time to clarify the stock. Garnish the matzo balls with gribenes and parsley.

Serves 4.

Consommé

Clarifying stock is worth the extra effort, especially if you're making the soup for special guests. The stock can be clarified up to 2 days before you want to serve it. The solid ingredients can be chopped by hand or everything can be puréed in a food processor, since they're all combined at the outset.

Consommé

1½ quarts/1.5 liters chicken stock

¾ pound/350 grams ground chicken thighs

½ Spanish onion, diced

1 carrot, diced

1 celery stalk, diced

1 bay leaf

3 large egg whites, plus the crunched-up eggshells (save the yolks for Sauce Baron, page 136, or for enriching Parisienne Gnocchi, page 121)

Combine all the ingredients in a 2-quart/2-liter pot (a narrow high-sided one is best) over high heat. Using a wooden spatula, stir the stock continuously, diligently scraping the bottom as you do to prevent the egg whites and meat from sticking and scorching. As the liquid gets hot and the protein congeals and rises to the top in what's called a "raft," it will begin to clarify the stock. Once the raft has formed, reduce the heat to low, so that a little of the stock is simmering up through cracks in or at the edges of the raft. Cook for 30 to 40 more minutes.

Disturbing the raft as little as possible, ladle or pour the stock through a strainer lined with a coffee filter into a serving bowl. Discard the beneficent raft.

The clarified stock can be refrigerated for several days, well covered, before using.

Yield: 1¼ quarts/1.25 liters clear stock

Pâté de Foie Gras en Terrine *with* Croutons

This recipe is almost identical to the traditional chopped liver recipe except that it calls for chicken fat reserved from roasted chicken, and it uses a food processor rather than a grinder or knife. Both changes were made to accommodate cooks who don't want to make or use schmaltz and don't have a grinder. (But, of course, feel free to use schmaltz and/or a grinder if that's what you wish.) This makes an impressive hors d'oeuvre, especially if you have an attractive terrine mold to

Pâté de Foie Gras en Terrine with Croutons

present the pâté with the elegance it deserves. To give this pâté an exceptionally smooth, clean texture, pass it through a tamis (a drum sieve) before putting it in the mold. Serve the pâté with water crackers or thin slices of toasted baguette or rye bread.

Pâté de Foie Gras en Terrine with Croutons

3 large eggs

¾ cup/180 grams melted chicken fat reserved from roasted chicken

1 Spanish onion, thinly sliced

1 pound/450 grams chicken livers

1 teaspoon kosher salt, plus more for sautéing the liver

1 teaspoon freshly ground black pepper

2 teaspoons red wine vinegar

Gribenes (optional)

Chives, finely minced (optional)

In a small saucepan, cover the eggs with an inch of water, and bring the water to a boil over high heat. When the water reaches a full boil, cover the pan and remove it from the heat. Let the eggs sit in the covered pan, off the heat, for 12 to 15 minutes, then remove them from the water.

Meanwhile, in a large sauté pan over medium heat, melt a third of the chicken fat, and cook the onion in it until completely tender and on the brink of browning, 10 to 15 minutes. Transfer the cooked onion to a plate.

Pâté de Foie Gras en Terrine with Croutons

Add a little more melted chicken fat to the pan, increase the heat to high, and sauté the livers, salting them as you do, until they are warm all through with just some pinkness remaining, 7 to 10 minutes.

Peel the eggs. If you have a ricer, rice the eggs into the food processor; otherwise, roughly chop the eggs and add them to the processor, along with the livers and onion, ½ cup/120 grams of the melted chicken fat, the salt, pepper, and vinegar, and process until smooth, scraping down the sides as needed. Taste the mixture and add more melted chicken fat, salt, pepper, and vinegar as you wish (remember that this will be served cold so it needs aggressive seasoning). Pass the mixture through a tamis if you want an exceptionally smooth texture. Press it into a terrine mold. Cover it with plastic wrap and chill completely.

Before serving, top it with gribenes and chives, if using.

Yield: about 2 cups/600 grams

Schmaltz-Roasted Potatoes with Onion and Rosemary

Potatoes cooked in animal fat—beef, pork, chicken, duck, or turkey—are superior to those cooked in vegetable fat. Something about these fats makes the potatoes especially crisp. Furthermore, the fat itself is deeply flavorful, and the potatoes absorb this flavor. For this reason, any kind of potato—from shredded potatoes for latkes or hash browns to French fries to leftover mashed potatoes—fried in schmaltz is fabulous. Here, the savory schmaltz combines with the rosemary and sweet onion to make a simple but delicious side dish.

Schmaltz-Roasted Potatoes with Onion and Rosemary

¼ to ⅓ cup/60 to 80 grams schmaltz

3 large russet potatoes, cut into medium dice (peel them if you wish)

1 Spanish onion, cut into medium dice

1 tablespoon freshly minced rosemary

Kosher salt and freshly ground black pepper

Put a heavy-gauge roasting pan or sturdy sheet tray in your oven and preheat the oven to 425°F/220°C.

Remove the pan from the oven and add the schmaltz (I speed the melting by putting the tray over a hot burner). Add the potatoes, stir to coat with the fat, and roast for 15 minutes. Add the onion and stir to coat. Return the pan to the oven and roast, stirring as necessary, until the potatoes are golden brown and crisp, another 30 minutes or so. Sprinkle the potatoes with rosemary and season with salt and pepper to taste.

Serves 6.

Chicken with Schmaltz Dumplings

Chicken with dumplings is one of the most delicious and comforting meals I know, especially on a cold night. It's also economical and easy, especially if you have excellent stock on hand. Good stock is key, so if you plan ahead and make some easy chicken stock from the carcass of a roast chicken, this is a meal that can be put together in 30 minutes.

Chicken with Schmaltz Dumplings

What makes this version so special are the elegant, airy dumplings. These are *pâte à choux*-based dumplings. *Pâte à choux* is an underused, all-purpose dough that's incredibly versatile: it makes *gougères* (cheese puffs), cream puffs, éclairs, and Parisienne gnocchi (a recipe for these follows). It's a great preparation to have in your repertoire. Water and butter are brought to a simmer; flour is added and quickly forms a paste. Eggs are beaten into the paste. The result can be baked, boiled, or fried, all to great effect. In this case, glorious schmaltz replaces the butter, but it's otherwise a traditional *pâte à choux* ratio: 2 parts each water and egg, 1 part each fat and flour. Fresh herbs are stirred into the *choux* for color and flavor.

You can use a number of different strategies to approach this dish. Here are two—one that assumes you have stock on hand (Version 1) and one completely from scratch, starting with a whole chicken (Version 2). I love the from-scratch method because it's a great way to utilize the whole chicken, but you need to make the stock from the chicken bones in advance, either early in the same day or up to 3 days before you intend to make the finished dish. A side benefit of making the stock in advance is that you can put the chicken skin in the freezer, which will make it easier to cut into small pieces. I recommend Version 2 for those who love to cook and have the time, and Version 1 for those who need to get a delicious, nourishing dinner on the table quickly.

Chicken with Schmaltz Dumplings 1
(quick and easy)

¼ cup/60 grams schmaltz

1 Spanish onion, cut into large dice

Kosher salt

1 or 2 carrots, peeled and cut into bite-size pieces

1 or 2 celery stalks, cut into bite-size pieces

3 or 4 boneless, skinless chicken thighs (8 to 12 ounces/240 to 360 grams total), cut into bite-size pieces (or use leftover cooked chicken, or roast the thighs first, then chop them)

¼ to ⅓ cup/35 to 45 grams all-purpose flour, depending on how thick you want your stew

Freshly ground black pepper

1 quart/1 liter chicken stock

1 recipe Parisienne Gnocchi, prepared up to the point where the dough is in the plastic bag (see page 121)

1 teaspoon white wine vinegar or lemon juice, or more to taste

Fresh tarragon, chives, or parsley, for garnish (optional)

In a large saucepan, heat the schmaltz over medium-high heat. Add the onion and an aggressive four-finger pinch of salt. Stir to coat with the fat, cooking for a minute or two. Add the carrots and celery and continue to cook for 5 to 10 minutes (don't burn them; reduce the heat to medium if necessary). Add the chicken. If using raw chicken, stir and cook till the chicken has lost all its color, about 5 minutes; if using cooked chicken, just stir briefly to heat it through.

Add the flour, stir to coat everything, and cook for a few more minutes. Give the meat and vegetables several grinds of pepper. Add the stock and stir continuously,

Chicken with Schmaltz Dumplings 1
(quick and easy)

scraping the bottom of the pan with a wooden spatula, until the stock thickens (turn the heat to high until it does, if you wish). When it begins to simmer, turn the heat down and let it cook for another 10 minutes.

Snip ½ inch/1.25 centimeters off one corner of the gnocchi bag and pipe the dough into the pot, cutting the dumplings off in 1½-inch/4-centimeter lengths. Cook until the dumplings are done, about 5 minutes. Stir in the vinegar or lemon juice and taste the liquid. If it needs more salt or pepper, add it. If it needs more acidity, add more vinegar or lemon juice. Serve, garnishing with fresh herbs if you have them.

Serves 4.

Chicken with Schmaltz Dumplings 2
(from scratch)

One 4-pound/1.8-kilogram chicken

2 Spanish onions, 1 roughly chopped and 1 cut into small dice

6 carrots, peeled, 4 roughly chopped and 2 cut into small dice

6 celery stalks, 4 roughly chopped and 2 cut into small dice

1 tablespoon black peppercorns

2 bay leaves

Kosher salt

¼ cup/60 grams schmaltz or butter (in addition to the schmaltz you'll make in this recipe)

1¼ cups/175 grams all-purpose flour

4 to 5 large eggs

¼ cup chopped fresh soft herbs (parsley, chives, tarragon, or chervil, or a combination)

Chicken with Schmaltz Dumplings 2
(from scratch)

Remove the skin and exterior fat from the entire chicken (you can leave the skin on the wings, if you wish; it's more trouble than it's worth to remove, in my opinion). If you're not planning to finish the dish right away, put the skin in the freezer. Remove both breasts from the bird and reserve (or freeze) for another use. Remove the leg-thigh pieces from the carcass and put them in a large pot. Break or chop the carcass into a few pieces so that it fits compactly in the pot. Add enough water to cover (about 2 quarts/2 liters), put the pot over high heat, and bring it to a boil.

While the water is coming up to heat, chop the skin into small pieces (this is easiest if it's frozen), put it in a small pot (nonstick, if possible) with a ¼ cup/60 milliliters of water, bring it to a simmer, and then cook over low heat. When the skin begins to brown—it can take 15 to 20 minutes depending on heat level—add about a third of the diced onion and continue cooking as directed in How to Make Schmaltz (page 11). You should end up with about ½ cup/120 grams schmaltz and ½ cup/60 grams gribenes.

Just as the pot with the chicken carcass begins to boil, copious foam and congealed protein will rise to the top. Scoop all this off with a spoon or a skimmer and discard. Reduce the heat to low and cook, just below a simmer, for 1 ½ hours. Transfer the leg-thigh pieces to a plate to cool. When they are cool enough to handle, pick off all the meat. Return the bones to the pot and continue cooking the stock for 2 to 4 more hours (the longer it cooks, the richer it will be). Roughly

Chicken with Schmaltz Dumplings 2
(from scratch)

chop the meat into bite-size pieces for your stew, cover, and refrigerate till you're ready to use.

Add the roughly chopped onion, carrots, and celery to the pot. Crack the peppercorns roughly, using a mortar and pestle or the bottom of a sauté pan. (Those who toast the pepper in a dry sauté pan before crushing get extra credit—this really brings out its flavor and is worth the effort.) Add the pepper, the bay leaves, and a four-finger pinch of kosher salt to the pot. Bring the temperature back up to just below a simmer, then reduce the heat to low and cook for another hour. Strain the stock through a fine-mesh strainer. You should have 1½ quarts/1.5 liters stock; if you have less than 1¼ quarts/1.25 liters, add enough water until you do.

To make the dumpling mixture, put 1 cup/240 milliliters of the stock into a small saucepan with the ½ cup/120 grams schmaltz you just made. Bring the stock to a simmer over high heat, then lower it to medium and add 1 cup/140 grams of the flour. Using a wooden spatula, stir the flour into the water until it forms a paste; this will happen quickly. Continue to stir for another minute or so to continue cooking the flour and cooking out some of the water.

Remove the pan from the heat and let it sit for 5 minutes, or hold the bottom of the pan under cold running water to cool it enough so that the eggs don't cook when you add them. Stir in one egg at a time until each egg is thoroughly incorporated (don't worry, they'll eventually blend in completely). Stir in the fresh herbs.

Chicken with Schmaltz Dumplings 2
(from scratch)

Invert a large zipper-top plastic bag over your hand and use it to gather up all the *pâte à choux*, then re-invert the bag with the *choux* inside. You will pipe this directly into your stew.

To finish your stew, combine the remaining ¼ cup/35 grams flour and the remaining ¼ cup/60 grams schmaltz (or butter) in a medium saucepan over medium heat and cook until the flour loses its raw aroma and begins to smell like pie crust, 2 minutes or so. Add the remaining diced onion and cook until the onion is wilted. Add an aggressive pinch of salt and many grinds of pepper. Add the diced carrot and celery and continue to cook, stirring, for another minute or two. Add 1 quart/1 liter of stock, whisking continuously, until the stock comes to a simmer and has thickened. Continue to cook it at a gentle simmer, stirring frequently to make sure the flour is not sticking to the bottom of the pan and scorching, 15 to 30 minutes, or as your schedule allows. Taste for seasoning and add more salt and pepper to your liking. Stir in the reserved chicken leg meat.

Snip ½ inch/1.25 centimeters off one corner of the plastic bag containing the *pâte à choux* and pipe the dumplings directly into the stew, cutting them off at 1½-inch/4-centimeter lengths. Cook the dumplings until they're done, about 3 minutes. If the stew is thicker than you like it, add more of the remaining stock until it reaches the consistency you wish. Serve in hot bowls.

Serves 4.

Parisienne Gnocchi with Spinach, Onion, and Poached Egg

The dumplings for chicken and dumplings are just too damn good to relegate to a single dish, so here is one that truly features them, enhances them by crisping them, and creates a fabulous, nourishing finished dish in minutes. It's best to make the dumplings ahead and let them cool; they can be tossed with oil or schmaltz and refrigerated for 3 to 4 days or frozen for a couple of weeks, then thawed.

Parisienne Gnocchi with Spinach, Onion, and Poached Egg

I first learned of Parisienne gnocchi while working on the *Bouchon* cookbook with Thomas Keller and Jeffrey Cerciello. In their research for restaurant dishes, they'd brought this excellent technique to the fore, and it remains a regular feature of the restaurants in Yountville, Las Vegas, and Los Angeles. When I read the recipe I thought to myself, *Wait a minute, this isn't gnocchi, it's* pâte à choux! *I didn't know you could boil it!* A revelation, and one that enhanced my respect for this incredibly versatile dough-batter hybrid that also gives us, when baked, *gougères*, cream puffs, and éclairs, or when deep-fried, *pets de nonne* (French doughnuts) and Mexican *churros*.

Traditional *choux* paste is made by simmering water and butter together, then adding flour, which absorbs the hot water and begins to gel, becoming a paste that "pulls away from the sides of the pan," as recipes invariably instruct. Whole eggs are then beaten into it one by one. The result is a dough/batter that puffs when you bake it. When you boil it, it takes on a pasta-like texture.

When working on this book, I thought, *Why not make* pâte à choux *using schmaltz instead of butter?* If you begin the dough with chicken stock instead of water, they're even more savory and flavorful. (And feel free to substitute matzo meal for the flour if you wish.)

Parisienne Gnocchi with Spinach, Onion, and Poached Egg

For this dish, the gnocchi are sautéed with onions in schmaltz till they're golden brown and crisp, spinach is wilted with them, and they are topped by that great all-purpose finishing ingredient, a poached egg. (For a beautiful poached egg, break the raw egg into a slotted spoon—or one of my Egg Spoons, available at http://shop.ruhlman.com—to let the loose white drop off before poaching it.)

Parisienne Gnocchi with Spinach, Onion, and Poached Egg

GNOCCHI:

1 cup/240 milliliters chicken stock or water

½ cup/120 grams schmaltz

1 teaspoon kosher salt

1 cup/140 grams all-purpose flour

4 to 5 large eggs

¼ cup chopped fresh soft herbs (parsley, chives, tarragon, or chervil, or a combination)

TO FINISH THE DISH:

2 tablespoons/30 grams schmaltz, or as needed

1 Spanish onion, halved crosswise and thinly sliced

1½ pounds/675 grams fresh spinach, stems removed

4 large eggs

Kosher salt and freshly ground black pepper

Make the gnocchi: Combine the stock, schmaltz, and salt in a medium saucepan over high heat. When the liquid reaches a simmer, lower the heat to medium and add the flour. Stir continuously until all the water has been absorbed and a uniform paste has formed. Continue to cook, stirring, for another minute or two. Set the pot aside to cool for 5 minutes, or hold the bottom of the pan under cold running water to cool it enough that the eggs don't cook when you add them.

Parisienne Gnocchi with Spinach, Onion, and Poached Egg

Crack an egg into the pan and quickly stir it to combine (it will be slick at first, but the paste will soon embrace the egg). Repeat with the remaining eggs (4 is standard, but 5 will make it richer). Stir in the herbs.

Bring a large pot of water to a boil (or use stock if you have it).

Invert a large zipper-top plastic bag over your hand and use it to gather up all the *pâte à choux*, then re-invert the bag with the *choux* inside. Snip ½ inch/ 1.25 centimeters off one corner of the bag and pipe the dough into the simmering water (or stock), cutting the gnocchi off at 1½-inch/4-centimeter lengths. When they float to the surface, they're done. Transfer them to a plate lined with a paper towel. Repeat with the remaining dough. Set the gnocchi aside or toss them with a little oil or schmaltz to prevent them from sticking together. Proceed with the rest of the dish immediately, or chill or freeze the gnocchi until you're ready to use them.

To finish the dish, bring a pot of water to a simmer for the eggs.

Meanwhile, in a large sauté pan, melt the schmaltz over medium heat, and sauté the onion until completely cooked (give it a little color but don't totally cook it down; you want some texture and bite). Add the gnocchi to the pan, along with

Parisienne Gnocchi with Spinach, Onion, and Poached Egg

more schmaltz if needed to help them to brown. They should turn an appealing golden brown after 4 or 5 minutes. When they look gorgeous, add the spinach.

Drop the eggs into the simmering water at this point as well, and reduce the heat to low. The eggs are poached when the white has completely solidified and the yolk is still fluid.

Meanwhile, finish cooking the spinach by gently tossing it with the gnocchi and onion until it's wilted. Give it all a pinch of salt and several grinds of pepper.

Divide the gnocchi and spinach among 4 warm plates, and top each with a poached egg. Give the eggs one last pinch of salt and a grind of pepper and serve.

Serves 4.

Chicken Confit

Confit, cooking and storing meat in its fat, is an age-old technique born of necessity (preserving enough food to eat through winter) that we continue to use because it results in such flavorful, succulent meat. It's most often associated with duck and goose, but it works fabulously well with chicken, although this is rarely done. It's best with the tougher, fattier parts of chicken, duck, and geese—that is,

Chicken Confit

the legs and thighs. For chicken, I like using the thighs because they're readily available at the grocery store and they pack nicely into the cooking vessel, reducing the amount of fat required. Of course, schmaltz is the fat of choice here, but pork fat or olive oil are excellent as well (I don't recommend vegetable oil or vegetable shortening because it adds no flavor to the confit).

As part of its preservation, confit was heavily salted; while we don't need all that salt now for practical reasons, we do need some for flavor. Aromatics are important in the cure as well. For duck confit, I like a simple garlic-thyme-pepper mixture, and that would work fine here, too. But I've ventured outside the traditional box here because I think that the mildness of the chicken responds well to a dynamic citrus-coriander combination. I also wanted to include the flavor of juniper berries but I didn't have any on hand, so I went with the next closest thing: gin. The orange and gin made me think of the Negroni cocktail, so I decided to add vermouth, too. It's important to cook the alcohol out of the gin and vermouth so that it doesn't denature the skin and meat of the chicken during its cure. The heat also helps to enhance the impact of the aromatics.

When the chicken thighs have been cooked and chilled in their fat, they can be reheated immediately, but the longer they're left to ripen in the fridge, the better they will taste. There will be an intensely flavored, salty stock at the bottom of the fat that becomes thick and gelatinous when chilled. I like to serve the crispy confit in a salad tossed with a sharp vinaigrette seasoned with this confit gelatin and shallots. The confit can also be used to make Chicken Rillettes (recipe follows).

Chicken Confit

½ cup/120 milliliters gin

¼ cup/60 milliliters sweet vermouth

1 tablespoon/15 grams kosher salt

2 tablespoons black peppercorns, lightly toasted and roughly cracked

2 tablespoons coriander seeds, lightly toasted and roughly cracked

4 or 5 garlic cloves, smashed with the flat side of a chef's knife

Zest from 1 orange, grated

8 chicken thighs or 4 leg-thigh pieces (about 1½ pounds/750 grams total)

2 to 4 cups/480 to 960 grams schmaltz (see note)

Note: This recipe calls for a lot of schmaltz. That's because this is a love song to schmaltz. But if you don't have access to lots of schmaltz and don't feel like shelling out for a batch of duck fat (which also works well), feel free to use olive oil, which is a great fat for confit.

Chicken Confit

Combine the gin and vermouth in a small saucepan over high heat. When it comes to a simmer, reduce the heat to medium, add the salt, pepper, coriander, and garlic and continue to cook until the alcohol has cooked off, a couple of minutes (hold a match or lighter to it—when the flame goes out, it's done). Remove the pan from the heat and allow the mixture to cool completely.

Place the chicken thighs in a plastic bag, a bowl, or a small baking dish. Add the zest to the cooled marinade and pour it all over the thighs. Rub it all around so that the chicken is evenly coated. Cover and refrigerate for 24 to 48 hours, rolling the chicken around in the marinade occasionally to redistribute the seasonings.

Preheat the oven as low as it will go—180°F/82°C is ideal, but 200°F/95°C is fine.

Rinse the chicken under cold running water to remove the marinade ingredients (if some of the coriander and pepper remain embedded in the skin, that's fine). Pat the thighs dry and place them in an appropriately sized baking dish that's safe for stovetop use; they should be well packed in so that you need as little precious schmaltz as possible. Cover the thighs completely with schmaltz (see note). Put the dish over medium heat on the stovetop until the fat reaches 180°F/82°C on an instant-read thermometer. Transfer the dish to the oven and cook for 8 to 10 hours. The confit has cooked long enough when the meat sinks to the bottom and the fat is clear; it's better to overcook than undercook.

Remove the dish from the oven. Allow it to cool, then cover and refrigerate it for at least 24 hours, and for up to 3 months. If you plan on keeping the confit thighs

Chicken Confit

for longer than a few days, be sure they are completely submerged in the fat, press a layer of plastic wrap down on the surface of the fat, then wrap the entire dish with foil—light is fat's enemy.

To reheat the confit, broil the thighs until the skin is crisp and they're heated through. Or, better, deep-fry them (preferably in strained schmaltz).

Yield: 8 chicken thighs

Chicken Rillettes

Rillettes are usually made from pork, or sometimes duck or even rabbit. The meat is cooked till it shreds easily, seasoned aggressively, moistened with fat, and served on croutons as an hors d'oeuvre. Sometimes I like to deep-fry chunks of the rillettes so that they're very crisp and serve them on a spinach or arugula

Chicken Rillettes

salad. Chicken rillettes are an excellent variation on this French charcuterie staple. Like a confit, chicken rillettes can be seasoned in any direction you wish—with herbs, Asian spices, or curry. Here, because I'm using the chicken from the confit recipe, I'm sticking with similar seasonings, adding more freshly ground black pepper, coriander, and orange zest, as well as some cumin. Marlene Newell, our chief recipe tester, suggested a step I recommend: For more flavor, broil the chicken to crisp the skin before mixing the rillettes.

Chicken Rillettes

4 confit chicken thighs, at room temperature or slightly warmed

1 teaspoon freshly ground coriander

1 teaspoon freshly ground black pepper

1 teaspoon finely grated orange zest, plus additional for (optional) garnish

1 teaspoon cumin seeds, toasted and ground, or ¾ teaspoon ground cumin

2 teaspoons sherry vinegar or red wine vinegar

Kosher salt

2 to 3 tablespoons schmaltz

Pull the meat and skin from the thigh bones (be careful not to include any carti-lage) and put it in the bowl of a standing mixer, larger mortar, or food processor with the remaining ingredients (start with a pinch of salt and a tablespoon or so of schmaltz). Paddle, pulverize, or purée the mixture till it forms a paste. Taste the mixture and add more seasonings if necessary.

Chicken Rillettes

Transfer the mixture to several small ramekins or one large dish. Smooth the top, pour a fine layer of schmaltz over the top to seal it, and garnish with orange zest if you wish. Cover with plastic wrap and store in the refrigerator for up to 10 days. Remove the rillettes from the refrigerator an hour or two before serving them; they should be at room temperature when eaten.

Yield: 2¼ cups/600 grams

Chicken *Suprêmes* with Sauce Baron

Chicken *Suprêmes* with Sauce Baron

Suprême refers to a cut of chicken that includes half of the breast with the drumette bone of the wing still attached. It's easy to do this yourself, but you can also ask your butcher or the butcher department of your grocery store to do it for you (it's also sometimes referred to as an "airline" cut).

This is an easy and delicious main course and easy to prepare, but the *raison d'être* for it is the schmaltz-based sauce, enriched and thickened with egg yolk and seasoned with tarragon, my favorite herb. To my knowledge there's no specific recipe like it, so in honor of Lois Baron, I'm calling it Sauce Baron, in French, given that it's basically a béarnaise sauce, using schmaltz instead of butter.

The sauce can be made in any of the ways you are accustomed to making emulsified butter sauces—using an immersion blender, a standing blender, or an old-fashioned whisk (which is my preference for the control it gives me). The schmaltz gives the sauce a wonderful depth of flavor that, with the shallot, lemon, and tarragon, is a perfect match for the chicken itself.

The following is a recipe for two, but it can, of course, be doubled. I recommend serving this with the Parisienne gnocchi, minus the poached egg because there's egg in the sauce (but if you love eggs, keep the egg!).

Chicken *Suprêmes* with Sauce Baron

2 chicken breast halves, *suprême* cut

Kosher salt and freshly ground black pepper

¾ cup/180 grams schmaltz

2 large egg yolks

1 tablespoon minced shallot

1 tablespoon lemon juice

2 teaspoons/10 milliliters water

Pinch cayenne

3 to 4 tablespoons chopped fresh tarragon

Season the chicken breasts aggressively with salt and freshly ground pepper 30 to 60 minutes before cooking them, and set them aside at room temperature.

Meanwhile, heat the schmaltz in the microwave till it's hot; spoon off about a tablespoon into a separate bowl and set aside. Combine the yolks, shallot, lemon juice, water, and cayenne in a bowl or a double boiler or saucepan. Whip the yolk mixture over medium-low heat (or over a pan of simmering water) for a few minutes,

Chicken *Suprêmes* with Sauce Baron

until the mixture is warm and fluffy. Whisking continuously, add the schmaltz, at first drop by drop, then in a steady stream until it's all incorporated. Remove the sauce from the heat and cover with plastic wrap.

Preheat the oven to 350°F/180°C.

Put an oven-safe sauté pan—one big enough to fit both chicken breasts—over high heat. When the pan is very hot, add the reserved tablespoon of schmaltz. When the fat is near smoking, lay the chicken breasts, skin side down, in the pan and leave them there for 3 to 5 minutes (don't even think about touching them). When the skin is golden brown and beautiful, turn them over (use a spatula, not tongs, to avoid tearing the skin; it should be crisp enough to have naturally separated from the pan), and slide the pan into the oven for another 5 minutes or until done (push on the fat part of the breast; it's nearly done if it still feels very soft; it's done when it gives just a little resistance but you can sense a little pinkness at the center; it's overdone if it's stiff, in which case you'll be especially glad for the sauce). You want it just past medium-rare. Remove the chicken from the oven and let it sit in the pan for 5 minutes.

Gently reheat the sauce over a low flame or water bath (or start-to-finish it now, while the chicken rests). Whisk in the tarragon. Spoon the sauce over the chicken, or make a pool of it on each plate and rest the chicken on the sauce.

Serves 2.

Chicken Sausage

This sausage uses chicken and schmaltz, along with plentiful sage, garlic, ginger, and pepper. And salt, of course—sausage needs salt. My optimal salt level is 1.75 percent, so I multiply the weight of the meat (in ounces or grams) by 0.0175 to get the amount of salt needed (also in ounces or grams). If you like less salt, take it back to 1.5 percent.

Chicken Sausage

This seasoning makes a great breakfast sausage as well as an excellent grilling sausage. If you have a sausage stuffer and like link sausage, by all means stuff this sausage into casing. I like to form patties and cook them either in a sauté pan or on the grill. The schmaltz can be replaced with pork fat or pork belly, if you have access to chicken thighs but not schmaltz, but I think it's most intensely flavored using chicken fat.

I'm fanatical about keeping sausage fixings cold all the way through the making, and I'm especially crazy about it here, because chicken fat is pourable at room temperature. Thus it's important to keep everything—the fat, the meat, and even the seasonings—close to frozen while you're making this. I freeze the fat, cut it into chunks, and then grind it frozen. After grinding, you can mix it by hand using a stiff spatula or wooden spoon, but a standing mixer with the paddle attachment works best. Either way, make sure the mixing bowl is cold.

Chicken Sausage

1½ pounds/675 grams chicken thigh meat, diced and thoroughly chilled

225 grams schmaltz, frozen (or a scant cup if you don't have a scale, but shame on you)

1 tablespoon/10 to 12 grams kosher salt

¾ cup roughly chopped fresh sage

2 large garlic cloves, finely minced

2 tablespoons finely chopped ginger

1 teaspoon freshly ground black pepper

½ cup/120 milliliters dry white wine, chilled

Combine all the ingredients except the wine in a large bowl and freeze for 20 to 30 minutes. Measure the wine and put that in the freezer, too. If your grinder attachment is metal, freeze that as well, and also your mixing bowl. Set up your grinder, remove the chicken mixture from the freezer, and grind it through a small or medium die into the freezing-cold mixing bowl. Return the meat to the freezer for 10 minutes and set up your stand mixer.

Chicken Sausage

Remove the sausage mixture from the freezer and mix it with the paddle attachment on medium high for 60 seconds or so, adding the very cold white wine as you do. Paddling will distribute the seasonings and give the sausage a good bind to help it hold together rather than crumble. In order to be sure the seasoning is right, fry a small portion of the sausage (put the mixing bowl in the fridge while you cook the test piece). Taste the test piece. If you think the mix needs more salt, pepper, sage, or ginger, add it and repaddle it. You can do this as often as you like till you get the seasoning just so.

Wrap the sausage in plastic wrap in the shape of a cylinder, about 2½ inches/ 7.5 centimeters in diameter. Put the wrapped sausage in a plastic bag. It will last a good week in the fridge (thanks to the salt) or 3 months in the freezer (the longer you freeze it, though, the more chance it has of getting freezer burn or picking up unpleasant freezer odors, so label the bag with the date and don't forget about it).

Yield: about 2 pounds/900 grams

Savory Brioche

Brioche is a special bread because of its delicate crumb, richness, and flavor. The traditional fat used is butter, but other cultures use lard. I propose one very good reason for using schmaltz instead of either: flavor! This is a delicious savory bread that makes superb dinner rolls to serve with chicken or turkey, a simple salad, chicken soup, or anything, really.

Savory Brioche

As far as I'm concerned, this version is out of the park (my assistant Emilia started it, I finished it, and our recipe tester Marlene tested it and confirmed). You need to make it the day before you bake it, but it's a really simple preparation. It can be baked free-form, in individual ramekins, or in a loaf or terrine mold. Marlene made nifty "bubble top" rolls by filling muffin cups with three 1-ounce/30-gram balls, a technique she picked up from Dorie Greenspan's excellent book *Around My French Table*. I had my first bite while it was still warm from the oven, with a little extra schmaltz and a sprinkling of Maldon sea salt. Heavenly. If you bake it in a rectangular mold, slice it and toast it—delicious.

This from Marlene: "OK, I want to say I was skeptical of this at the beginning. The dough smelled chickeny, not only while it was rising but also while it was baking. However, these totally rocked. There was no hint of chicken in the taste or the smell in the final product. The crust is the best I've ever produced. It was crisp, almost flaky, like biscuits. The crumb was delicate and soft."

Savory Brioche

⅓ cup/80 milliliters milk

2 tablespoons/30 grams honey

1 teaspoon/5 grams instant yeast

14 ounces/400 grams all-purpose flour (about 3 cups)

3 large eggs

½ cup/120 grams room-temperature schmaltz

1½ teaspoons/8 grams kosher salt

Oil, butter, or additional schmaltz for greasing the pan

Combine the milk, honey, and yeast in the bowl of a standing mixer fitted with a dough hook (this can also be done by hand in a large bowl if you don't have a mixer). Turn the mixer on to distribute the yeast. Add the flour and turn the mixer to medium speed. Once the flour has begun to absorb the liquid, add the eggs, one at a time. When the eggs are incorporated add the schmaltz, then the salt, and mix on high until all the ingredients are well incorporated, 3 to 5 minutes.

Savory Brioche

Cover the mixing bowl with a lid or with plastic wrap and let the dough ferment and rise till it's doubled in size, about 3 hours (less if your kitchen is hot).

Grease your cooking vessel (see below).

Reknead the dough by hand to redistribute the yeast and knock some of the gas out. Shape as desired: form into balls and place in a cake pan or springform mold for dinner rolls, or in individual ramekins or a muffin pan, or put the whole dough ball as is in a terrine mold or loaf pan. Cover loosely with plastic wrap and refrigerate for 8 to 36 hours.

Remove the dough from the refrigerator 1½ to 2 hours before baking (shorter if they're in individual portions, longer if a single loaf). Preheat the oven to 350°F/180°C. When the dough has reached room temperature and has started to rise, bake it. Individual portions will take about 25 minutes, whole loaves about 45 minutes. If you're uncertain about doneness, insert an instant-read thermometer—the brioche is done when it's reached an internal temperature of 200°F/95°C. The crust should be an appealing golden brown.

This dough can also be frozen after the fermentation stage. Shape or mold it, wrap twice in plastic, and freeze. To bake the dough, refrigerate it for 24 hours, then allow it to temper and rise at room temperature for 2 hours before baking.

Yield: one 2-pound/900-gram loaf, 9 bubble-top rolls, or 12 dinner rolls.

Scones with Roasted Red Pepper and Parmigiano-Reggiano

Scones with Roasted Red Pepper and Parmigiano-Reggiano

These scones were conceived and developed by Emilia, our colleague in schmaltz, when we were looking for new ways to use this flavorful fat. I am not generally a fan of scones because they are so often heavy and dry, but these are amazingly moist and light! My favorite scones ever. Emilia smartly chose to add a colorful garnish of sun-dried tomatoes. I wanted something moister, and used chopped roasted red pepper and some onion that I'd cooked in schmaltz. Fabulous. One of our chief testers, Barbara, chose to use oven-dried Roma tomatoes. Another, Dana, used caramelized onion. They all work great! This is one of my favorite schmaltz preparations in the book. With a salad, they make a great meal. Or they're a terrific side dish for a stew or any braise. These have made me a complete scone convert.

Scones with Roasted Red Pepper and Parmigiano-Reggiano

2 cups/280 grams all-purpose flour, plus more for dusting

½ teaspoon/3 grams kosher salt

1 tablespoon/15 grams baking powder

¾ cup/180 milliliters buttermilk

2 large eggs

6 tablespoons/15 grams grated Parmigiano-Reggiano

½ cup/90 grams any or all of the following: chopped roasted red pepper, chopped sun-dried tomato, oven-roasted tomato, diced onion sautéed in schmaltz

¼ cup/60 grams schmaltz, well chilled or frozen

Preheat the oven to 400°F/200°C.

Combine the dry ingredients in a mixing bowl.

Combine the buttermilk and 1 egg in a separate bowl and blend thoroughly. Stir in 3 tablespoons of the Parmigiano-Reggiano, and the pepper, tomato, and/or onion.

Cut the cold schmaltz into the flour mixture or squeeze it into pea-sized pieces as if making a crust.

Scones with Roasted Red Pepper and Parmigiano-Reggiano

Add the buttermilk mixture to the dough and mix just till it comes together. Dump it out onto a well-floured surface and pat into a disk about 8 inches/21 centimeters in diameter and 1 inch/3 centimeters thick. If it's very wet, dust the top with flour. Cut the disk into wedges and place them on a baking sheet, either nonstick or lined with parchment paper or a silicone baking mat. The scones can be baked immediately or double-wrapped in plastic and frozen for up to 2 days, and then baked straight out of the freezer.

Before baking, whisk the remaining egg till it's uniformly blended. Brush the scones with this egg wash and top with the remaining 3 tablespoons Parmigiano-Reggiano.

Bake for 13 to 15 minutes if at room temperature, 20 to 25 minutes if frozen. They should be golden brown and hot all the way through.

Yield: 8 scones

Oatmeal Cookies with Dried Cherries

That's right: schmaltz oatmeal cookies. We had to have something sweet! The schmaltz does have a great effect here—it doesn't make the cookie taste like chicken, but it does give it a savory depth to balance the sweetness. Using schmaltz in a cookie turns out to be a fascinating and useful example of balancing sweet and savory ingredients. I love the tart, dense dried cherries in these cookies, but this recipe is a great all-purpose vehicle for whatever spin you want to give them— raisins, dried cranberries, walnuts, pecans, or a mixture of any of the above.

Oatmeal Cookies with Dried Cherries

¾ cup/180 grams schmaltz, well chilled or frozen

½ cup/150 grams granulated sugar

½ cup/120 grams packed brown sugar

1 large egg

1 teaspoon/5 grams pure vanilla extract

1½ teaspoons/3 grams cinnamon

1 teaspoon/5 grams kosher salt

1½ cups/150 grams all-purpose flour

1 teaspoon/4 grams baking powder

2 cups/200 grams old-fashioned oats (not quick-cooking)

⅔ cup/85 grams dried cherries or other interior garnish (see page 152 for suggestions)

Oatmeal Cookies with Dried Cherries

Preheat the oven to 350°F/180°C.

Cut the schmaltz into chunks and put it, along with both sugars, into the bowl of a standing mixer fitted with the paddle attachment. Mix on high until the fat is fluffy, 2 minutes or so.

Add the egg, vanilla, and cinnamon and mix on low to incorporate.

Combine the salt, flour, and baking powder, and add this to the mixing bowl. Paddle on medium to combine, 30 seconds or so. Add the oats and paddle to combine. Add the garnish and paddle to combine.

Shape the dough into golf ball–sized orbs and place on a cookie sheet. Flatten them to your desired thickness (they won't spread much, but they will puff). Bake the cookies until done, about 15 minutes.

Yield: about 18 cookies

Chicken Stock

Chicken Stock 1
(all-purpose)

This is an all-purpose chicken stock recipe to use when you've saved up a lot of miscellaneous bones in the freezer, or if you have access to lots of raw chicken carcasses.

Chicken Stock 1
(all-purpose)

2 pounds/900 grams raw chicken bones

3 quarts/3 liters water, or more if necessary

½ pound onion, chopped

½ pound carrot, chopped

¼ pound celery, chopped

1 bay leaf

1 teaspoon black peppercorns, crushed with the bottom of a sauté pan

2 to 3 sprigs fresh thyme

2 to 3 sprigs fresh parsley

2 to 3 garlic cloves, peeled

Put the bones in a 6-quart/6-liter stockpot and cover them with the water. Put the pot over high heat and bring the water to a simmer. Skim the foam and congealed protein off the surface. Reduce the heat to low and cook for 4 hours (or place in an oven preheated as low as it will go—180°F/82°C is ideal, but 200°F/95°C is fine, too). Add the remaining ingredients; they will cool the stock. Bring it back up to just below a simmer, 180°F/82°C or so, and continue to cook for another 45 minutes to an hour.

Discard the bones and strain the stock through a fine-mesh strainer; for an even better result, strain again, using a kitchen cloth or cheesecloth.

Yield: 2½ quarts/2.5 liters

Chicken Stock 2
(from a whole raw chicken)

One good strategy for ensuring that you always have chicken stock on hand is to buy a single chicken as a multitasking ingredient. Here's how the chicken is broken down: The breasts are reserved for another meal. The legs and thighs are cooked through but removed when just done. The wings and carcass finish the stock. With the resulting 1½ quarts/1.5 liters of stock, you can make soup, chicken and dumplings, or whatever you wish. You can pick the meat off the bones and add it to the stock for soup, or reroast it to crisp the skin and serve with Schmaltz-Roasted Potatoes with Onion and Rosemary (page 111).

Chicken Stock 2
(from a whole raw chicken)

One 4-pound/1.8-kilogram chicken

2 quarts/2 liters water, or more if necessary

1 Spanish onion, roughly chopped

2 carrots, roughly chopped

2 bay leaves

1 teaspoon black peppercorns

1 tablespoon/18 grams tomato paste

A few smashed garlic cloves, whole sprigs of parsley and thyme (optional)

Cut the breasts off the carcass, wrap, and refrigerate or freeze for later use. Separate the entire leg from the carcass at the joint. Cut the wings from the carcass at the joint. Chop or break the carcass into 3 or 4 pieces so that it fits in the pot.

Put the carcass, legs, and wings in a 3-quart/3-liter saucepan, cover with the water, and place over high heat. As soon as the water reaches a boil, turn the heat to low. Skim and discard the foam and congealed protein that rise to the top.

After 1 hour, remove the legs, allow them to cool, and refrigerate until you want to use them. If you know you're going to be taking the meat off the bones eventually, do it as soon as they are cool enough to handle, then return the denuded bones and cartilage to the stockpot.

Chicken Stock 2
(from a whole raw chicken)

Continue cooking the stock for 3 more hours. Add the remaining ingredients. Raise the heat to bring the liquid back to a simmer, then reduce it to low and cook for 1 more hour.

Discard the bones and strain the stock through a fine-mesh strainer; for an even better result, strain again, using kitchen cloth or cheesecloth.

Yield: 1½ quarts/1.5 liters stock, 2 fully cooked chicken legs, 2 breasts ready to be cooked

Chicken Stock 3
(from a roasted chicken carcass)

This is my go-to stock for most weeks of the year, made from the remains of a roasted chicken. I finish it in the oven to ensure that it has had plenty of time in gentle heat. It's easy—you just stick it in the oven and forget about it. If you forget about it for too long, though, you may need to add more water before adding the vegetables.

Chicken Stock 3
(from a roasted chicken carcass)

1 roasted chicken carcass (and any leftover pieces or bones that have not been dispatched)

1½ quarts/1.5 liters water, or more if necessary

1 Spanish onion, roughly chopped

2 carrots, roughly chopped

2 bay leaves

1 teaspoon black peppercorns

1 tablespoon/18 grams tomato paste

A few smashed garlic cloves, whole sprigs of parsley and thyme (optional)

Preheat the oven as low as it will go—180°F/82°C is ideal, but 200°F/95°C is fine.

Break the chicken carcass into pieces. Put the bones and any leftovers in a 3-quart/3-liter oven-safe saucepan and cover with the water. Bring it to a simmer over high heat on the stovetop. When it reaches a simmer, put the pan in the oven for at least 4 hours and as many as 12 hours (I simply put mine in the oven and let it cook overnight).

Chicken Stock 3
(from a roasted chicken carcass)

Add the remaining ingredients, bring the stock back to a simmer over high heat on the stovetop, then return the pan to the oven for another hour or hour and a half.

Discard the bones and strain the stock through a fine-mesh strainer; for an even better result, strain again, using kitchen cloth or cheesecloth.

Yield: about 1 quart/1 liter stock

I. Mise en place for making stock from assorted raw or cooked chicken bones: bones, aromatic vegetables, and seasonings.

→

2. Cook your stock over low heat. The pot should be too hot to hold your fingers against, but the water should be relatively still. →

3. Don't boil your stock as above—not if you want it to remain translucent and clean-tasting. It's not a tragedy if you boil it (and sometimes it is desired for speed and to emulsify the fat into the liquid), but as a rule, stock is best when it's cooked gently.　→

4. After the bones have cooked, add the vegetables.

→

5. Add more water to cover, if necessary. →

6. Let the water temperature come back up. →

7. The vegetables need to cook for about an hour in the stock.   →

8. Strain the stock through a fine-mesh strainer. →

9. Discard the carcass and vegetables, which will have given all their flavor to the liquid.   →

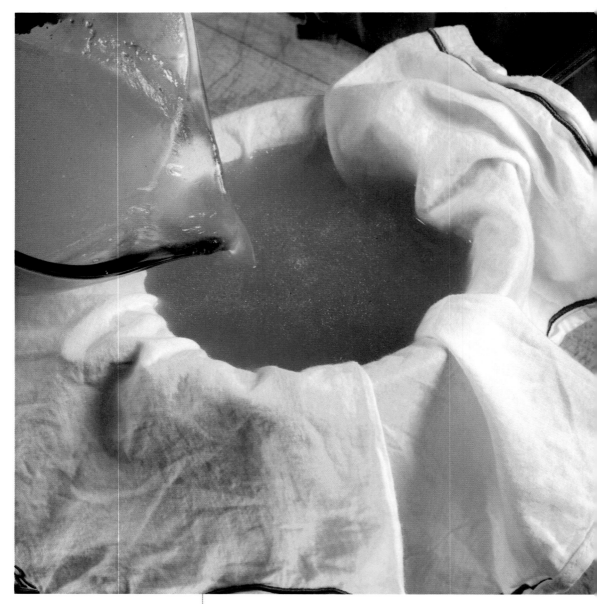

10. For a more refined stock, strain it again, this time through a kitchen cloth.

ACKNOWLEDGMENTS

I set this experimental project into motion, but it wouldn't have gone far without the help of many people. As the opening remarks note, Lois Baron gave me the push I needed to explore schmaltz.

My wife and partner, Donna Turner Ruhlman…well, this wouldn't be happening at all without her to photograph the food in her clean, journalistic style. When I told April (see below) what schmaltz was, April nodded blankly (she'd never heard of it before). But then, when I showed her my iPad with Donna's process shots of schmaltz being made, her eyes brightened. "Ah, *now* I understand!" Thank you, Donna, for capturing my ideas as images. Your photography helps countless people to *understand*. Donna was also the driving force behind the move to self-publish this book as an iPad app first. Thanks for that as well.

Phong Nguyen designed the iPad app this book is based on, and April Clark of Nuance Consulting and Will Turnage, a vice president of technology and invention at the digital advertising company R/GA, assisted with the digital conversion. This work was not intended to be a hardbound book until Little, Brown editor Michael Sand—a visionary, I have no hesitation in saying—thought of making it so. I owe him and Little, Brown many thanks.

Marlene Newell oversaw the testing of all recipes. Not easy given that she'd relocated to Calgary, Canada, where many of the ingredients were hard to come by. Marlene and I also relied on Barbara Laidlaw, Dana Noffsinger, and Emilia Juocys to retest and comment on recipes on Marlene's site, CooksKorner.com.

I was lucky to chance on a fine copyeditor, Boston-based Karen

Wise, whose work behind the scenes on my prose and recipes is excellent in its invisibility. She also provided valuable insight into Jewish cookery and culture generally. Thank you, Karen.

And finally, Emilia Juocys, my Chicago-based assistant, who is much more than an assistant—cook, competitive curler, recipe developer, and personal motivator. Thank you, Emilia.

Thank you, all!

INDEX

Page numbers in *italics* refer to instructional photos.

ABOUT THE AUTHOR

Michael Ruhlman's innovative and sucessful food reference books include *Ratio, The Elements of Cooking, Ruhlman's Twenty,* and *Charcuterie.* He has appeared as a judge on *Iron Chef America* and as a featured guest on Anthony Bourdain's *No Reservations.* He has also coauthored books with prominent chefs, including Thomas Kellar, Eric Ripert, and Michael Symon. He lives in Cleveland with his wife, photographer Donna Turner Ruhlman.

Donna Turner Ruhlman has photographed for many books, including *Ratio* and *Ruhlman's Twenty,* and is the sole photographer for her husband's blog, Ruhlman.com.